Last Stand at Mobile

CIVIL WAR CAMPAIGNS AND COMMANDERS SERIES

Under the General Editorship of Grady McWhiney

PUBLISHED

Battle in the Wilderness: Grant Meets Lee by Grady McWhiney

Death in September: The Antietam Campaign
by Perry D. Jamieson

Texans in the Confederate Cavalry by Anne J. Bailey

Sam Bell Maxey and the Confederate Indians by John C. Waugh

The Saltville Massacre by Thomas D. Mays

General James Longstreet in the West: A Monumental Failure
by Judith Lee Hallock

The Battle of the Crater by Jeff Kinard

*Cottonclads! The Battle of Galveston and the Defense of the
Texas Coast* by Donald S. Frazier

A Deep, Steady Thunder: The Battle of Chickamauga
by Steven E. Woodworth

The Texas Overland Expedition by Richard Lowe

Raphael Semmes and the Alabama by Spencer C. Tucker

War in the West: Pea Ridge and Prairie Grove by William L. Shea

Iron and Heavy Guns: Duel Between the Monitor and Merrimac
by Gene A. Smith

The Emergence of Total War by Daniel E. Sutherland

John Bell Hood and the Struggle for Atlanta by David Coffey

*The Most Promising Young Man of the South: James Johnston
Pettigrew and His Men at Gettysburg* by Clyde N. Wilson

Vicksburg: Fall of the Confederate Gibraltar
by Terrence J. Winschel

This Grand Spectacle: The Battle of Chattanooga
by Steven E. Woodworth

Rutherford B. Hayes: "One of the Good Colonels"
by Ari Hoogenboom

Jefferson Davis's Greatest General: Albert Sidney Johnston
by Charles P. Roland

*Unconditional Surrender: The Capture of Forts Henry
and Donelson* by Spencer C. Tucker

Last Stand at Mobile by John C. Waugh

Last Stand at Mobile

John C. Waugh

Under the General Editorship of Grady McWhiney

McWHINEY FOUNDATION PRESS
McMURRY UNIVERSITY
ABILENE, TEXAS

Library of Congress Cataloging-in-Publication Data

Waugh, John C.
    Last stand at Mobile / John C. Waugh ;under the general
    editorship of Grady McWhiney.
    p. cm.—(Civil War campaigns and commanders series)
    Includes bibliographical references (p.) and index.
    ISBN 1-893114-08-2
    1. Mobile (Ala.)—History—Civil War, 1861-1865—
Campaigns. 2. United States—History—Civil War, 1861-1865—
Campigns. 3. Mobile Bay (Ala.), Battle of, 1864. I. McWhiney, Grady.
II. Title. III. Series.

F334.M6 W38 2001
973.7'54—dc21   2001052210
                                                              CIP

Printed in the United States of America

ISBN 1-893114-08-2
10 9 8 7 6 5 4 3 2 1

Book Designed by Rosenbohm Graphic Design

All inquiries regarding volume purchases of this book should be
addressed to McWhiney Foundation Press, McMurry Station, Box 637,
Abilene, TX 79697-0637.
Telephone inquiries may be made by calling (915) 793-4682

www.mcwhiney.org

A Note on the Series

Few segments of America's past excite more interest than Civil War battles and leaders. This ongoing series of brief, lively, and authoritative books—*Civil War Campaigns and Commanders*—salutes this passion with inexpensive and accurate accounts that are readable in a sitting. Each volume, separate and complete in itself, nevertheless conveys the agony, glory, death, and wreckage that defined America's greatest tragedy.

In this series, designed for Civil War enthusiasts as well as the newly recruited, emphasis is on telling good stories. Photographs and biographical sketches enhance the narrative of each book, and maps depict events as they happened. Sound history is meshed with the dramatic in a format that is just lengthy enough to inform and yet satisfy.

Grady McWhiney
General Editor

CONTENTS

1. Waiting at the Gates — 13

2. On the Brink of Battle — 23

3. "Damn the Torpedoes!" — 35

4. Hellfire in the Harbor — 49

5. Fall of the Forts — 61

6. March of the Yankee Columns — 68

7. Showdown at Spanish Fort — 78

8. Sunset on the Gulf — 86

Appendix A — 90

Appendix B — 91

Appendix C — 92

Further Reading — 104

Index — 111

CAMPAIGNS AND COMMANDERS SERIES

Map Key

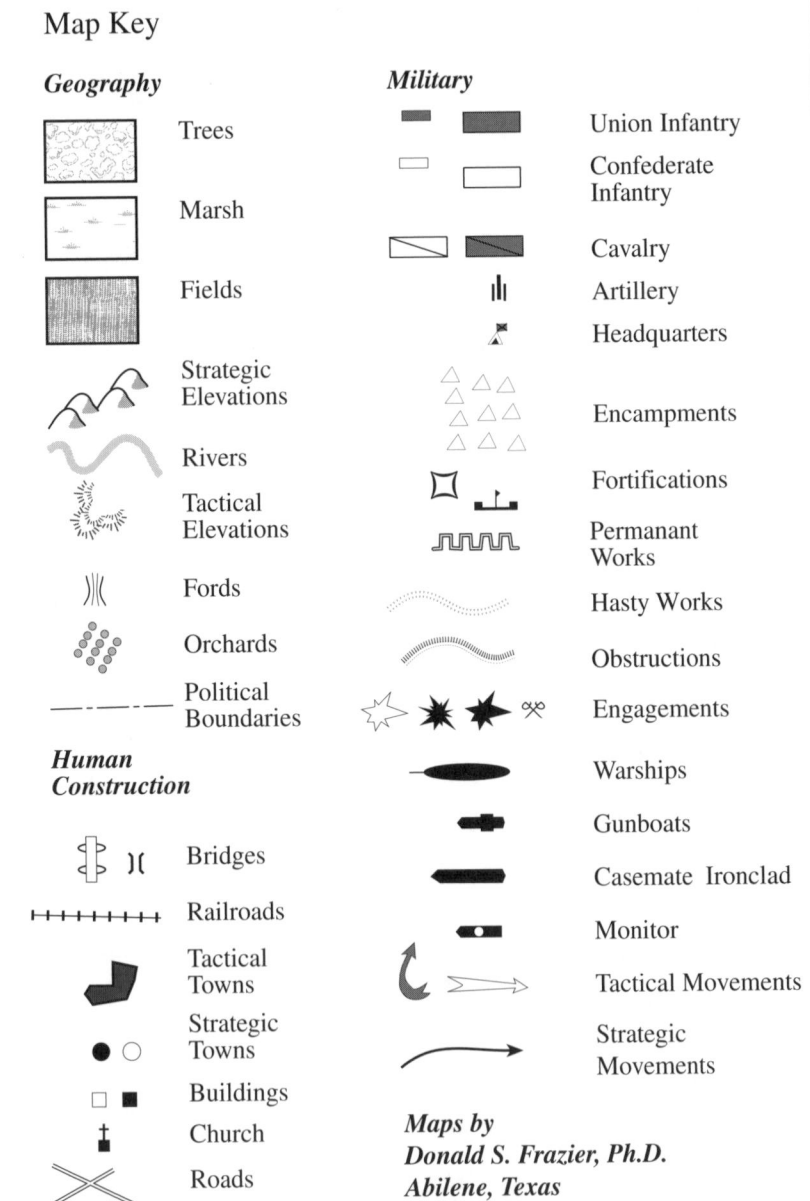

Geography

Trees

Marsh

Fields

Strategic Elevations

Rivers

Tactical Elevations

Fords

Orchards

Political Boundaries

Human Construction

Bridges

Railroads

Tactical Towns

Strategic Towns

Buildings

Church

Roads

Military

Union Infantry

Confederate Infantry

Cavalry

Artillery

Headquarters

Encampments

Fortifications

Permanant Works

Hasty Works

Obstructions

Engagements

Warships

Gunboats

Casemate Ironclad

Monitor

Tactical Movements

Strategic Movements

Maps by
Donald S. Frazier, Ph.D.
Abilene, Texas

MAPS

The Defenses of Mobile   17

The Fleets at Mobile Bay   33

"Damn the Torpedoes"   39

Flight of the Rebel Gunboats   47

Capture of the *Tennessee*   58

PHOTOGRAPHS AND ILLUSTRATIONS

David Glasgow Farragut	14
CSS *Tennessee*	21
USS *Hartford*	25
David Farragut and Gordon Granger	27
Thornton Alexander Jenkins	28
David Farragut and Percival Drayton	30
James Alden	32
Percival Drayton	36
Tunis Augustus MacDonough Craven	41
James Edward Jouett	43
Franklin Buchanan	51
James D. Johnston	53
The *Hartford* Engaging the *Tennessee*	54
Surrender of the CSS *Tennessee*	59
Gordon Granger	62
Richard Lucian Page	64
Dabney Herndon Maury	69
Edward Richard Sprigg Canby	72
Frederick Steele	74
Andrew Jackson Smith	75
Union Troops Entering Mobile	87
Richard Taylor	88

Last Stand at Mobile

1

WAITING AT THE GATES

The admiral's orders to his fleet were as taut as an anchor chain in a swift-running tide, as ominous as the gleaming howitzers frowning from his flagship's gun deck: "Strip your vessels and prepare for the conflict. Send down all your superfluous spars and rigging. . . . Put up the splinter nets on the starboard side, and barricade the wheel and steersmen with sails and hammocks. Lay chains or sand bags on the deck over the machinery, to resist a plunging fire. Hang the sheet chains over the side, or make any other arrangement for security that your ingenuity may suggest."

They were orders for battle, fighting orders: "The vessels will run past the forts in couples, lashed side by side. . . . The flagship will lead . . . and the others . . . will follow in due order until ordered to anchor."

They were precise orders that told the captains of his fleet how they must fight: "[The ships]" will open fire the moment the enemy opens upon us. . . . Use short fuzes for the shell and shrapnel, and as soon as within 300 or 400 yards give them grape. . . . The howitzers must keep up a constant fire from the time they can reach with shrapnel until out of its range."

They were orders that expected trouble and allowed for it: "If one or more of the vessels be disabled, their partners must carry them through."

It was July 1864, and for two years Union rear admiral David Glasgow Farragut had yearned to issue these orders. That was how long he had wanted to storm the defenses of Mobile Bay, since the spring of 1862, after he had run the forts at New Orleans and taken that queen of Southern port cities. Seizing this last major remaining Confederate harbor

DAVID GLASGOW FARRAGUT

David Glasgow Farragut: born Tennessee 1801; after moving with his family to New Orleans, came under the guardianship of Capt. David Porter; in 1810, not yet ten years old, appointed midshipman in the U.S. Navy; the following year joined Porter's crew aboard the frigate USS *Essex;* serving in the Pacific during the War of 1812, appointed prize master of a captured British vessel; actively engaged during Porter's defeat by two British warships at Valparaiso; taken prisoner and exchanged in November 1814; next five years spent on duty mostly in the Mediterranean; studied in Tunis and in 1825 became a lieutenant; thereafter saw a variety of duties in the Gulf of Mexico and the south Atlantic; in 1841 promoted to commander; the following year took command of the sloop USS *Decatur;* largely left out of the action during the Mexican War; given command of the sloop USS *Saratoga* but arrived too late to participate in the capture of Veracruz; varied assignments, and promotion to captain, followed; at the outbreak of the Civil War, was awaiting orders at his home in Norfolk, Virginia; moved family to New York after Virginia's secession; initially along the Gulf of Mexico had been his priority.

"Had I my own way," he wrote the assistant secretary of the navy, Gustavus Vasa Fox, in December 1862, "it would be to attack Mobile first & then have my whole available force free for the [Mississippi] River & Texas & the Rio Grande." In early 1863 he had written, "I would have had it long since, or been thrashed out of it."

But the powers in Washington had other plans. They had wanted first to conquer the Mississippi and if possible to win Texas. That had been the War Department's priority in the Gulf, and the admiral had to do it their way, not his.

Mobile itself was too well fortified. Farragut knew that. He realized his fleet could not get within shelling distance of the

viewed with suspicion as a Southerner, his only assignment in 1861 was as a member of the retirement board; in January 1862 became commander of the West Gulf Blockading Squadron with the mission of capturing New Orleans; the city fell in April 1862 after the bulk of Farragut's fleet ran past Forts Jackson and St. Philip on the Mississippi River and captured the defenseless city in what may have been the most decisive single action of the war—one from which the Confederate government could not rebound; rear admiral, June 1862, for this action; moved his fleet up the Mississippi and, in July 1862, fought past the Vicksburg batteries before returning to the Gulf of Mexico; again ascended the Mississippi to attack Port Hudson in March 1863; in July of that year, returned to New York and received a hero's welcome; returning to the Gulf in January 1864, began preparing for operations against Mobile; in August 1864 launched attack against Confederate forces in Mobile Bay by running past Forts Morgan and Gaines; while aboard his flagship, USS *Hartford*, is reported to have exclaimed "Damn the torpedoes, full speed ahead" while leading the fleet beyond the forts and through a mine field; in December, suffering from poor health, returned to New York, where citizens presented him with $50,000 for the purchase of a house in the city; vice admiral, December 1864; returned to duty in the waning days of the war and was among the first Federal officers to enter Richmond after its fall. After the war he commanded the European Squadron and in July 1866 became the first full admiral in the nation's history. Admiral Farragut died at Portsmouth, New Hampshire, in 1870, still on active duty in his sixtieth year of service with the U.S. Navy.

city, bristling with forts and batteries and shielded by the torpedo-laden waters of an upper bay too shallow for the drafts of his men-of-war. But he could at least attempt to pass the forts at the mouth of the bay, isolate them from the city, occupy the bay's deeper lower waters, and close the harbor to Southern blockade runners.

That would not be easy, even for this admiral, the U.S. Navy's harbor-storming specialist. It would test all of his daring, judgment, and skill. But in his mind it was the least he could do. Such a conquest would be a bracing morale booster for the Union cause—a victory at the end of a melancholy summer for Federal arms, a summer that had been expected to bring the defeat of Gen. Robert E. Lee's Army of Northern Virginia before Richmond and the fall of Atlanta in the West but had brought neither.

The conquest of Mobile Bay would at least be something, a very big something. It would assure Farragut's ocean-tossed West Gulf Blockading Squadron a safe and quiet anchorage, deny the same to Confederate blockade runners, and make possible the eventual conquest of the city itself.

Now, in this summer of 1864, Washington had finally given Farragut the ships, the firepower, an army division to help reduce and capture the forts, and the green light. He had issued his orders to his fleet. He was waiting at the gates. It was about to happen at last.

Mobile, the second ranking of the great cotton ports of America (eclipsed only by New Orleans), was one of the most beautiful cities of the South, situated on high and rolling ground on the shore of one of America's most commodious bays. Its system of roads paved with oyster shells and its varied and striking vegetation gave Mobile a special charm, and its thirty thousand residents gave it life. It was a water-girt city resting on a many-channeled delta. Not only was it fronted by its enormous bay but two great rivers, the Alabama and the

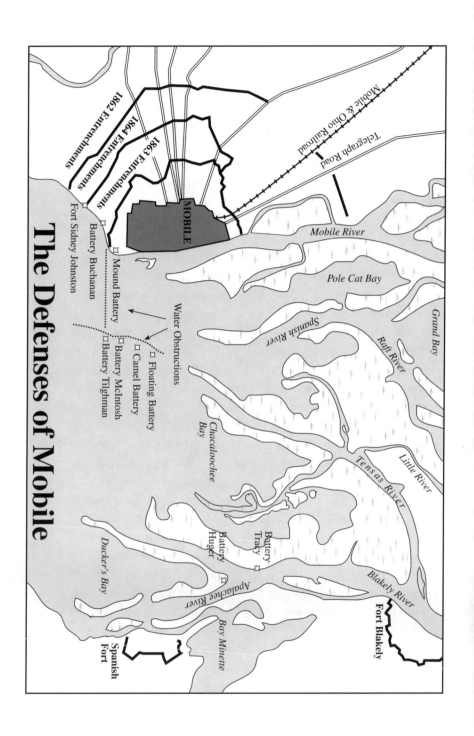

The Defenses of Mobile

Tombigbee, also flowed toward it from the interior, interlinked in their approaches by multiple branches. Their waters emptied into the bay through the Mobile River to the west and the Apalachee to the east.

Not only was Mobile one of the South's premier ports but it was also a strategic rail center and the best-fortified city in the Confederacy, untouched as yet by battle. During nearly four years of civil war, its defenses had been constantly strengthened and upgraded. In 1862 a continuous line of earthworks, including fifteen redoubts (reinforced breastworks), was built three miles west of the city on ground 150 feet above the Mobile River. After the fall of Vicksburg in the summer of 1863, a second line with sixteen more strong redoubts was constructed nearer the city. Yet a third line of defense, midway between the first two, was in the making, with nineteen forts and eight redoubts of nearly impenetrable strength, parapets twenty feet thick, and ditches twenty feet deep and thirty feet wide. The defenses had, in fact, outstripped the capacity of the Confederate soldiers on hand to man them. It would take forty thousand men to do the job adequately, a force the Rebels could never hope to muster.

The approach to the city by way of the bay was blocked by ten batteries on the shore, on islands, and on floats. Elaborate pile obstructions in shallow water laced with deadly torpedoes supplemented the batteries. An assault on the city from the bay was impractical. An advance overland from the north was out of the question. An attack from the west appeared just as futile. Only a land invasion from the east held any promise for a successful Union conquest. And that had to be over an old bastion called Spanish Fort, some twelve miles from the city, and past another work, Fort Blakely, five miles closer in. If fortified, as surely they would be, they would be formidable obstacles.

Union army engineers conceded, therefore, that Mobile was virtually impregnable to direct assault. Though they had long coveted the city, they had been unable to puzzle out how to take it. The only sensible way seemed to be to compel its evacuation, which would first require control of the bay and then a monstrous demonstration of force.

The bay fronting Mobile was thirty miles long, measured from its upper reaches inland to its mouth at the Gulf. Its width varied from six to fifteen miles, and the depth throughout its greater part was twelve to fourteen feet, shelving gently at the shorelines. At the Gulf entrance was a deep pocket extending from the mouth of the bay north-northwest for six miles, having an average width of two and a half miles and a depth of twenty to twenty-four feet.

The principal access to the bay was directly from the Gulf between the tip of a long, low finger of land, called Mobile Point, projecting from the mainland on the east and Dauphin Island to the west. The distance between these two points was nearly three miles. The main channel itself closely skirted Mobile Point, narrowing at the entrance to a funnel less than two thousand yards wide. This snug, well-corked harbor had long been a haven for Confederate blockade runners—"carrier doves" the Southern women called them because they brought into the Confederacy coveted goods from the world beyond the bay, in return carrying out its precious exports of cotton.

Two forts, Morgan and Gaines, guarded the bay's narrow entryway. Fort Morgan on Mobile Point, looming dark and menacing over the main shipping channel, was the bigger, stronger, and more strategically situated of the two. It was an old masonry bastion, built, a visitor once said, "in the old style, with bricks here, there, and everywhere." Morgan was a five-sided work, greatly fortified against assault by stacks of sandbags shielding every part of its exposed front. Within its walls were two tiers—a casemate and barbette level—mounting about forty-five guns of assorted calibers. Another fifteen guns were mounted in exterior batteries, the most formidable in a water battery fronting the fort. About half of this arsenal bore directly on the channel. Within its walls was a citadel, loopholed for musketry and manned by a garrison of six hundred officers and men. Fort Morgan's gun barrels were within pointblank range of the narrow channel through which Admiral Farragut must run his invading fleet. The Confederates had tried to make this work impregnable and the channel it guarded impassable—they were banking on it.

Fort Gaines, the other position guarding the entrance to the bay was not a factor against Farragut's assault. Lying three miles to the west on Dauphin Island, it was a small, star-shaped brick and earthwork fortification mounting a few heavy guns, none near enough to the main ship channel to make a difference. It did not enter into Farragut's calculations. Neither did Fort Powell, a third, much smaller earthwork on Tower Island, commanding the approach to the bay from Mississippi Sound, about six nautical miles northwest of Fort Gaines. This approach admitted only very light draft vessels and was thus impractical for a mighty seagoing fleet.

Entering strongly into Farragut's calculations, however, other than the guns of Fort Morgan, was the danger planted in the channel itself and waiting in the waters beyond.

The channel was laced to within a few hundred yards of the shore with a bristling bed of torpedoes, floating mines anchored to the bay bottom and daunting to the life and spirit of any sailor. Some of these engines of destruction were merely beer kegs filled with powder and triggered to explode on contact with the hull of a passing vessel. Most, however, were tin cones fitted with caps and capable of blowing a hole twelve by eight feet square in the bottom of the average wooden-hulled boat and sinking it almost instantly.

Some 180 torpedoes had been planted in the bay in anticipation of Farragut, for the Confederates had been expecting him for a long time. The torpedoes ran in a triple line to within 225 yards of the water battery under Fort Morgan. Through that narrow channel, left open for the "carrier doves," the admiral intended to pass his men-of-war.

CSS *Tennessee*

If Farragut did manage to negotiate these mind-numbing land and water obstacles and gain the harbor, worse was waiting within.

Not much of a Confederate fleet existed anywhere in 1864. But a little flotilla under Adm. Franklin Buchanan was waiting in Mobile Bay. Three of this tiny squadron's boats were small paddle wheelers, unarmored except around their boilers. One of these, the *Selma*, was a converted mail packet. The other two, the *Morgan* and the *Gaines*, were built for the Confederate navy but poorly put together, lightly constructed, and lightly armed. These three gunboats also counted for little in Farragut's calculations.

But there was another ship waiting there in the bay, Buchanan's flagship, the *Tennessee*, and it counted mightily. The *Tennessee* was the most powerful ironclad built by the Confederacy from the keel up. It was 209 feet long and 48 feet at the beam, drawing 14 feet of water fully gunned and loaded. Its hull armor was plated iron five to six inches thick. Its outside decks were sheathed in two-inch-thick plates. Its vicious iron ramming beak, projecting like a giant horn just below the waterline, was capable of systematically sinking every ship in Farragut's wooden-hulled armada. If this was not daunting enough, the *Tennessee* carried on her gun deck two 7-inch and four 6.4-inch long-range Brooke rifles that fired shot weighing

95–110 pounds. She was a death-dealing machine, looking, thanks to her sloping superstructure, like a monstrous snapping turtle with, as one visitor observed, "many a dark-looking corner" within.

She had been built in Selma on the Alabama River in the winter of 1863–64, and as soon as her frame was in place, she had been towed to Mobile to be armed and armored. But as powerful and daunting as this great screw-driven boat was, she had an Achilles heel—two of them actually. Like all Civil War ironclads, she lacked speed—six knots maximum—and her steering chains, instead of being led under her armored deck, were snaked over it, exposed to enemy fire—an appalling piece of unfortunate engineering. Only by luck could she overtake a swifter prey, and at any moment she could lose her steering.

The *Tennessee* was a flawed monster, but she was the best Confederate hope at Mobile. And she was waiting in the bay beyond the guns of Fort Morgan, beyond the bed of torpedoes, for Admiral Farragut's fleet.

2
ON THE BRINK OF BATTLE

David Farragut seemed made by the gods for this kind of work. When the war came, he was in his sixtieth year and had been in the navy nearly half a century. He was thoroughly qualified and more than ready for the job at hand.

In the summer of 1864, he was a fit sixty-three years old, of medium height, (about five feet, six inches tall), and weighed not over 150 pounds. His complexion was sallow and swarthy, bespeaking his descent from Spanish grandparents on his father's side. Farragut could in no way be called handsome. His face was oval, his cheekbones prominent, his eyes were hazel, his nose aquiline, his lips small and compressed. The admiral bore himself always erect because, as he often declared, he could not afford to lose a fraction of his scanty height. Though bald on the top of his head, his black hair, turning white about the temples, was permitted to grow long on the left side and carefully brushed over the bare spot—"the after guard . . . made to do foc's'le duty," as the sailors put it.

While Farragut might thus hide his bald spot from the world, to conceal his feelings was more difficult for him, and when deeply moved, impossible. One of his young officers described him as a "sprightly, kind, mild, and pleasing gentleman," yet with a "lion-like character and presence when battle was going on." That officer thought the admiral a "contrast between sunshine and storm." Another of his young officers said, "I think Farragut was the pluckiest man I ever knew . . . absolutely insensible to fear." And a third said, "his crouch is as careful and stealthy as the panther, and his leap as sudden and deadly."

Farragut was Tennessee-born. His mother had died of yellow fever when he was only seven, and he never saw his father after he was nine, the age at which he was given to the sea as a midshipman in the navy. He was only twelve years old during the War of 1812, and for a time at that tender and callow age he had briefly captained a vessel.

Committed to a life at sea, he had little formal schooling. But in his sixty-three years, he had learned to speak—besides English—French, Italian, Spanish, and Arabic.

Farragut was as sound in body as he was fluent in tongues. He delighted in physical exercise and was one of the finest swordsmen in the service. The admiral invariably wore his saber ashore, and when returning to the dark and deserted wharves at night through the low parts of town, he was ready and able to defend himself, believing that anyone wearing a sword ought to be ashamed not to be able to use it.

He often spoke in maxims: "If once you get in a soldier's rear, he is gone." "The more you hurt the enemy, the less he will hurt you." "The *best* protection against the enemy's fire is a well-directed fire from our own guns." "I believe in celerity." All that he thus preached he had practiced at New Orleans, and now he intended to employ them at Mobile Bay.

The flagship in which he planned to lead his fleet past the

USS *Hartford*

guns of Fort Morgan was as worthy and battle tried as the admiral himself—if not as sea worn. The steam sloop USS *Hartford* was five years old, commissioned in 1859. She was a top-of-the-line man-of-war, one of the premier vessels in the Union navy. A 1,900-ton screw ship, *Hartford* was 225 feet long, her greatest breadth of beam being 44 feet, with a mean draft of 16 feet. Her engines were capable of eight knots, and under steam and sail combined, she could make eleven. Already in her short existence she had been hit 240 times by shot and shell. Like the admiral, his flagship was by practice a fort-storming specialist—and shot and shell were what such a specialty invited.

The waiting had been far more wearing on Farragut over the past few months than battle would have been. He had whiled away the first half of the year in the monotonous routine of the blockade, rocking on the waves outside the bay with only his wooden ships, unable to get either ironclad monitors, which he must have to deal with the CSS *Tennessee,* or the necessary army support.

"If any one asks what I am doing," he wrote home in early April, "answer, Nothing but waiting for the world to turn round till it comes to my turn to do something, and then I will 'pitch in'; but I am like cold sauce, always ready."

Every day of waiting allowed the Confederates to strengthen their defenses inside the bay, making an assault ever more deadly. The Rebels had worked at fever pitch during these first months of the year to get the *Tennessee* armed and into position. The ram drew too much water to cross the shallow Dog River bar on its own and had to be lifted over on floats—called "camels" by the sailors—made fast to its sides.

As the Confederates labored with the *Tennessee* and continued to seed the channel with yet more torpedoes, Farragut could only wait, watch, and wish orders to attack would arrive.

The ram made Dog River bar and appeared in the waters of the lower bay quite suddenly on May 20. Since then, both sides had expected the worst. Rebel naval commander Franklin Buchanan expected Farragut to storm the channel any day. Farragut expected any dark night that Buchanan would run to the open sea in his hulking ram with its lethal iron beak and attack the wooden hulls of his fleet.

"I am tired of watching Buchanan," Farragut wrote home in late June, "and wish from the bottom of my heart that Buck would come out and try his hand upon us. . . . Anything is preferable to lying on our oars." But he had no choice, for the army was still occupied in the Red River campaign in Arkansas and Texas and he still lacked ironclads. In July both the army and the ironclads began arriving, and Farragut began laying his plans and issuing his orders.

The fleet would steam past the forts, skirt the torpedo bed, capture or destroy the *Tennessee*, and isolate the forts and cut off all possible avenues of escape. During the assault, his four ironclads were to take position between the fleet and Fort Morgan to keep down the fire from the water batteries and the parapet guns and to attack the *Tennessee* as soon as the fort was passed.

The old admiral's kinship with these *Monitor*-style, flat-

David Farragut and Gordon Granger

decked Union ironclads was a love-hate affair. Basically, he did not like them. "Give me hearts of iron in ships of oak," he sometimes said. But Farragut knew he needed them; for months he had begged for them. Now he had been promised two from the Atlantic fleet—the USS *Tecumseh* and the USS *Manhattan*—and two from the Mississippi fleet, the USS *Chickasaw* and the USS *Winnebago*. All four vessels were screw ships with poor speed, only five to seven knots, but they

THORNTON ALEXANDER JENKINS

Thornton Alexander Jenkins: born Virginia1811; though making preparations to attend college, when the time came for the decision he chose to join the military; midshipman, U.S. Navy, 1828; less than a year later, performed heroically in the breaking up of pirate groups in Cuba; from 1834 to 1842, worked with Prof. Ferdinand R. Hassler on the coastal survey; lieutenant, 1839; spent a year in Europe studying delicate coast-control operations provided an in-depth report in 1845; at the beginning of the Mexican War served as executive officer of the USS *Germantown;* commanded the landing of his ship's troops during the capture of Tuxpan and Tabasco; also saw duty in the West Indies during the late 1840s; in 1850 elected secretary of the first temporary lighthouse board and served for two years; then appointed secretary of the permanent lighthouse board, holding that post until 1858; at the request of Pres. Abraham Lincoln, he served on this board again in 1861-62; captain, July 1862; served as senior officer during two engagements a month later, Coggin's Point and City Point on the James River; commanded USS *Oneida* during the blockade of Mobile Bay later that year; flag captain, 1863, and command of the USS *Hartford*, campaigning on the Mississippi River under the orders of Adm. David Farragut; in 1864 took command of the USS *Richmond* and the second division of Farragut's fleet off Mobile Bay; from 1865 to 1869 served as chief of the Board of Navigation; commodore, July 1866; rear admiral, July 1870; commanded Asiatic Squadron until his retirement in 1873. Jenkins resided in Washington, D.C., until his death on August 9, 1893.

were sheathed with that wonder armor, iron. They could fight the *Tennessee* on an equal footing. And they were on the way.

There was not enough army to attack both forts at once, so Farragut had worked out an understanding with Maj. Gen. Gordon Granger, commanding the army division sent to help him. As the fleet entered the bay, Granger's troops would land on Dauphin Island and invest Fort Gaines. Powerful Fort Morgan would have to be squeezed into submission later.

Farragut had sent one his most trusted captains, Thornton Jenkins, commanding the *Hartford*'s sister ship USS *Richmond*, to Pensacola to complete the outfitting of the squadron that was to attempt to run the forts. Now fifty-two years old, Jenkins was a favorite not only of Farragut but also of Franklin Buchanan. He had been a midshipman under Buchanan in the "old navy" and later a first lieutenant in a corvette under him during the Mexican War. Jenkins had commanded the *Hartford* when Farragut passed the Port Hudson and Grand Gulf batteries in March 1863. He had been seasoned in fire. To him now fell the duty of getting the ships of the armada, particularly the ironclad *Tecumseh*, which had not yet arrived from the Atlantic, into line and ready for the fight.

On August 1, Dr. Daniel B. Conrad, the fleet surgeon of the Confederate squadron, aboard the *Tennessee* looked out beyond the harbor to the open Gulf and noted that the size of the waiting Federal fleet had ballooned. Through his glass he saw that the frigates were stripped to a "girt line" and cleared for action, their decks devoid of all extra rigging. They looked to him like prizefighters ready for the ring. The doctor sensed that trouble lay ahead and was very likely coming soon.

The sailors in the Federal fleet also sensed it. "Guess we are going to fight soon," Charles Brother, a marine private aboard the *Hartford,* speculated in his journal on August 2. "Everything is being got ready for fighting and I guess a few more days will tell whether we are to take Mobile or not."

That same day Percival Drayton, Farragut's fleet captain and skipper of the *Hartford,* wrote Jenkins in Pensacola inquiring when the *Tecumseh* could be expected, for Farragut was growing impatient. "I don't believe the admiral will wait much longer," Drayton warned his brother officer, "but go in with the force he has, which will get in if any can." The next day Drayton wrote Jenkins again, even more urgently: "I think a very little persuasion would have taken him in to-day, and

David Farragut and Percival Drayton

less to-morrow. . . . You had better come out if you want to be sure of a place in the fight."

While Drayton prodded Jenkins, General Granger landed his troops on Dauphin Island. Farragut was mortified. He had not held up his end of the agreement, being unable to go in simultaneously with his fleet, which was not yet all there.

"I have lost the finest day for my operations," he wrote Jenkins. "The soldiers, by agreement, are landing to-day back of Dauphin Island, and could I have gone in this morning, we would have taken them [the Confederates] by surprise. . . . I can lose no more days. I must go in day after to-morrow morning at daylight or a little after. It is a bad time, but when you do not take fortune at her offer you must take her as you can find her."

Meanwhile, Dr. Conrad took particular note of the three monitors now standing in with the Federal fleet. "Strange-looking, long, black monsters," he described them, lying so low in the water that the smoke from their smokestacks "appeared to come out of the ocean itself."

As the troops began landing, a detachment of army signal officers came aboard the ships of the Union fleet. They were to advise General Granger when the armada had passed the forts. Assigned to the *Hartford* was Lt. John Coddington Kinney of the 19th Connecticut Infantry.

Private Brother wrote in his journal that Farragut and Drayton had that afternoon sent all their valuables off the ship. That was the final tip-off. "Guess we will get some hard knocks and that pretty soon," he wrote.

Just before sunset on August 4, the *Tecumseh* arrived outside the harbor, escorted by the *Richmond.* Silently, ominously, she dropped anchor beside the three other ironclads in the lee of Sand Island, three miles from Fort Morgan. Farragut's final missing piece was in place.

"The report is that we are going to fight tomorrow morning," Private Brother told his journal. "Guess we are. God grant that we may have good luck."

Farragut was counting on more than luck. He wanted and expected two favors from nature: one, a westerly wind the next morning to blow the smoke from his guns toward Fort Morgan to hide his fleet from Rebel view; the other, a flood tide to carry any crippled ship on into the bay as well as straighten the mooring lines of the dreaded torpedoes and turn their primers away from the hulls of his approaching fleet. He knew he would have the tide; he did not know if he would have the wind.

JAMES ALDEN

James Alden: born Maine 1810; midshipman, U.S. Navy, 1828 on board the USS *Concord;* in 1838 joined Wilkes's South Sea expedition; lieutenant, 1841; during the Mexican War saw action at Veracruz, Tuxpan, and Tabasco; later took an active role in the Indian war on Puget's Sound; in command of the steamer USS *South Carolina* at the start of the Civil War; helped reinforce Fort Pickens, Florida, and saw action at Galveston, Texas; commander of USS *Richmond,* seeing action at the passage of Forts Jackson and St. Philip and during the campaigns to capture New Orleans and Vicksburg; captain, 1863; commanded the USS *Brooklyn* during the battle of Mobile Bay in August 1864; his hesitation at the sight of the USS *Tecumseh* sinking reportedly prompted Admiral Farragut's famous declaration "Damn the torpedoes! Go ahead!" as he drove the USS *Hartford* onward; with the *Brooklyn* participated in the two attacks on Fort Fisher during the closing months of the war; commodore, 1867; appointed chief of the Bureau of Navigation, 1869; rear admiral, 1871, and assigned the command of the European Squadron. Rear Admiral Alden retired from the navy at that rank and resided on the West Coast until his death on February 6, 1877.

At the urgent request of the captains and commanding officers of his armada, Farragut had made one adjustment in his orders: the *Brooklyn,* not the *Hartford,* would lead the fleet into the bay. *Brooklyn,* a sister ship of the flagship, had four chase guns, more than any other vessel in the fleet, and an ingenious arrangement on her bow called a "cowcatcher" or "torpedo catcher" for picking up mines. The van would be in good hands. James Alden, the fifty-four-year-old captain of the *Brooklyn,* a direct descendent of the Mayflower pilgrim John Alden, had been chief of the coast survey in antebellum days and author of the official charts of Mobile Bay. He was a skilful

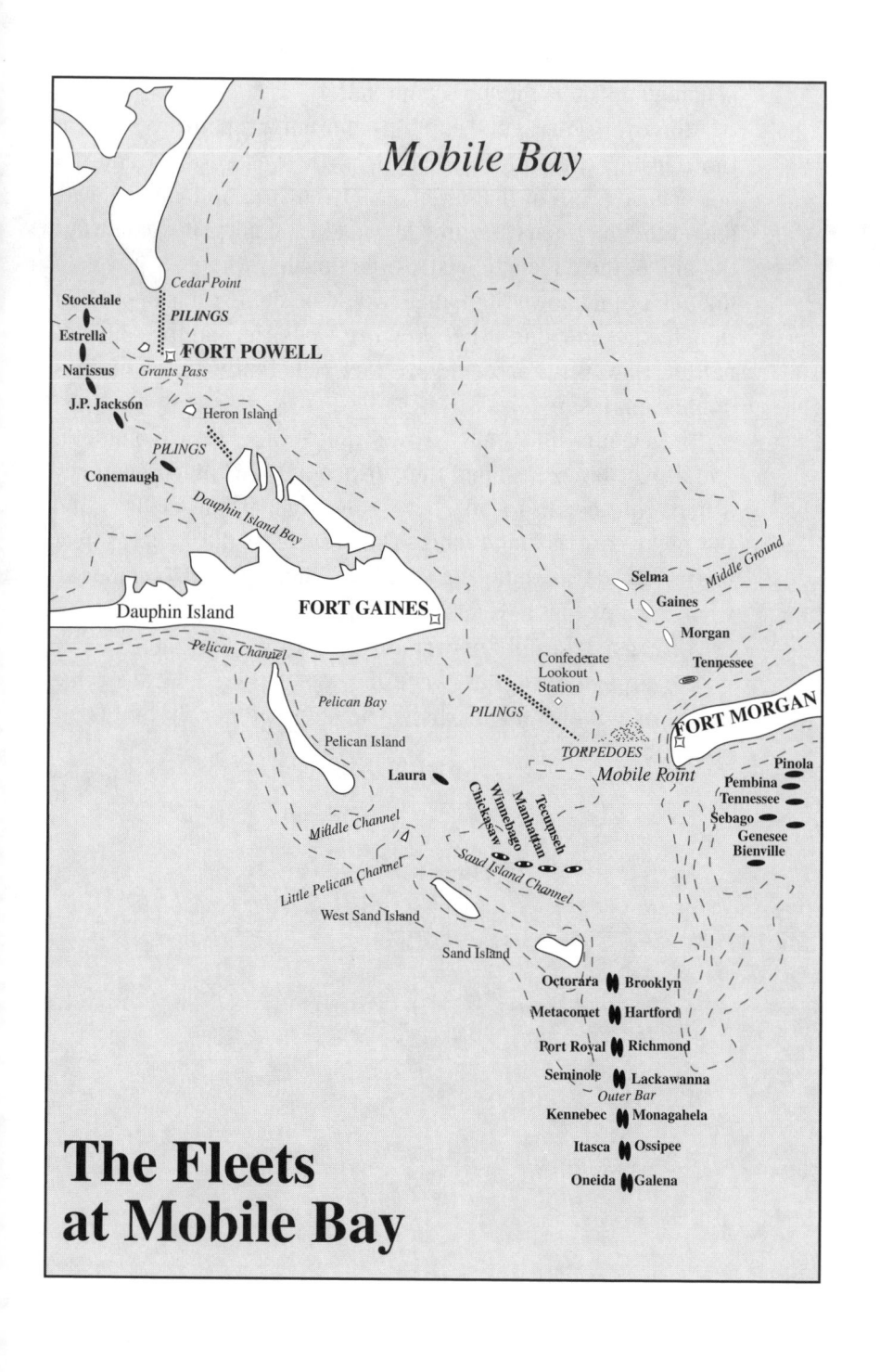

The Fleets at Mobile Bay

seaman and knew the harbor intimately.

Moreover, Farragut's captains did not want to overexpose the flagship carrying their admiral. He was dubious and did not believe at all in this argument. Exposure, he believed, was one of the necessary hazards of rank in the navy. It was always the aim of the enemy to destroy the flagship wherever it was in line, and God knows the Rebels would be doing their best to do that in the morning. The *Hartford's* position simply did not matter. However, Farragut gave way, reluctantly, to the urgings of his captains.

The evening of August 4 was quiet, the sea was smooth, and a light breeze rippled the surface of the Gulf. At sundown a hard rain began to fall, but by midnight it had cleared and the night grew hot and calm. The vessels of the Federal fleet lay quietly at anchor, the monitors inside Sand Island, the wooden ships just beyond.

Farragut had only one more thing to do, one more loose end to tie before battle—write his wife, Virginia. "I am going into Mobile Bay in the morning," he informed her, "if God is my leader, as I hope He is."

3
"DAMN THE TORPEDOES!"

The admiral slept fitfully during the night. He was feeling unwell. At about three o'clock in the morning, he sent his steward to test the wind. When he returned and reported a light breeze from the southwest, Farragut knew that nature, at least, favored the day.

"Then we will go in this morning," he said.

A peculiar dance was soon underway in the Gulf as the men-of-war and the gunboats began pairing up. At 4:30 A.M. the USS *Metacomet*, a side-wheeler and the fastest gunboat in the fleet, drew alongside the *Hartford* and was lashed fast. Two by two, the other vessels linked up, the smaller gunboats lashed to the port sides of the larger ships of the line according to Farragut's orders, the better to survive the plunging fire from Fort Morgan—the *Brooklyn* with the *Octorara*, the *Richmond* with the *Port Royal*, the *Lackawanna* with the *Seminole*, the *Monongahela* with the *Kennebec*, the *Ossipee*

PERCIVAL DRAYTON

Percival Drayton: born South Carolina 1812; parents William Drayton and Ann Gadsden were part of a distinguished and aristocratic family; attended the New York Naval School; was appointed midshipman, U.S. Navy, at age fifteen; served successfully in the Brazil, Pacific, and Mediterranean Squadrons and later received ordinance duty at the New York Navy Yard; commander, 1855; three years later assigned to aid Commodore Shubrick, commanding the Brazil Squadron and Paraguay expedition; stationed at the Philadelphia Naval Yard on ordinance duty at the outbreak of the Civil War; sympathetic with the North, on February 25, 1861, requested that the naval register acknowledge his Philadelphia residency; given command of the USS *Pocahontas* in October 1861 and participated in Capt. Samuel Du Pont's expedition against Port Royal, South Carolina; after proclaiming that his devotion to the North was so strong that he would rather sacrifice every relative he had no matter how painful it would be than interfere with the success of the Union, his native state of South Carolina declared and proscribed him as infamous; active with the South Atlantic Blockading Squadron and in reconnaissances of St. Helena Sound and adjacent waters; present at the capture of Fernandina and St. Mary's and at the occupation of the Stono River; captain, monitor USS *Passaic*, 1862; participated in bombardment of Fort McAllister and received commendation for his role in the attack of Fort Sumter; was appointed fleet captain in December1863 over the West Gulf Blockading Squadron, commanding the flagship USS *Hartford;* participated in the operations against Confederates at Mobile Bay; with the reputation of an exemplary officer with expertise in organizing and administration, appointed chief of Bureau of Navigation in April 1865. Almost four months later, after a few days illness, Captain Drayton died on August 4,1865, in Washington; to honor him, the U.S. Navy named the torpedo boat USS *Drayton* after him.

with the *Itasca,* and the *Oneida* with the *Galena.*

At 5:30 A.M., Farragut was sipping the last of his morning coffee. Turning to his fleet captain, Percival Drayton, the admiral said, "Well, Drayton, we might as well get under way."

Farragut said that in English, but he might just as well

have said it in Arabic or any of the other languages he spoke, for Drayton would have understood. Not yet fifty-two years old, Drayton was thought of navywide as the beau ideal of a naval officer. Tall and commanding, a South Carolinian by birth, he was endowed with exceptional mental powers, ranking high as a naval scholar, and like his admiral, fluent in several languages. Drayton was a crack seaman and a gifted organizer and administrator. And he was just as eager for this day and this battle as Farragut himself.

On a smooth sea under an unclouded sky, the ships of the fleet began to swing two by two into their assigned positions in line and then steam at a steady pace down the main ship channel toward the bay. The drums pounded in the soft early morning light—drum answering drum, from man-of-war to man-of-war, from the head of the line to the rear—in a hoarse summons to quarters. The four monitor ironclads, lying low in the water, slowly swung into position to the starboard of the line, the *Tecumseh* in the lead abreast of the *Brooklyn*.

It was nearly six o'clock and day was breaking. Aboard the *Tennessee* in the waters just beyond Fort Morgan, the quartermaster descended the ladder to Admiral Buchanan's cabin and in his gruff voice said: "Admiral, the officer of the deck bids me report that the enemy's fleet is under way."

Up on deck, Buchanan turned to the ram's skipper, Cmdr. James D. Johnston, and said: "Get under way Captain Johnston; head for the leading vessel of the enemy, and fight each one as they pass us."

The little four-vessel Confederate flotilla—the ram and its three gunboats—moved out from behind Fort Morgan into the open bay and took position in a single line en echelon across the channel, black smoke pouring from their funnels and their port batteries bearing on the approaching Union fleet. "It was a beautiful sight to see the enemy's fleet standing in towards Fort Morgan with all their colors flying," one of the *Tennessee*'s officers admitted. "I never beheld such a sight since I was born."

At 6:47 A.M., the first shot—fired by the *Tecumseh*—shattered the morning quiet. It was not a shot in anger; the ironclad was calibrating her guns. Quickly, she reloaded them with sixty pounds of powder and steel shot, making ready to engage the *Tennessee.*

The gunners in Fort Morgan had been expecting Farragut's move for several nights and had been sleeping on the ramparts as they waited. They now watched as the awesome armada steamed toward them, drawing ever nearer. The crews ignored the *Tecumseh*'s calibrating shot. But just after seven o'clock, when the fleet was less than a mile out, now within range, Brig. Gen. Richard Lucian Page, commanding the garrison, turned to J.W. Whiting, his officer of the day, and said, "Open the fight, sir."

The first shot in anger thundered from Morgan's guns toward the fleet at 7:06 A.M. From the channel, the *Brooklyn* answered in kind.

Within minutes, shell, shrapnel, grape, and canister were hissing through the air from both directions. It seemed to William F. Hutchinson, an assistant surgeon on the *Lackawanna,* "as if hell itself had broken loose." The fleet was "vomiting fire from stem to stern" from its broadside guns, and the fort was replying. The din was so deafening that orders had to be screamed to gunners only three feet away.

As the fleet passed into this iron storm, smoke from its guns began to rise in ever higher billowing clouds, shrouding the entire scene as Farragut had hoped it would. Gunners in the fort could no longer see their targets. The wind across the field of fire was doing its job. "Many a heart on our side sent up a prayer of thanksgiving for that breeze," the Union army's M.D. McAlester later wrote, "and doubtless many a rebel heart was filled with curses upon it."

As the smoke thickened and rolled, the doughty Farragut began climbing the port main rigging to get above it. Higher and higher he climbed until finally he was in the futtock

"Damn the Torpedoes"

Mobile Bay

Middle Ground

Selma

Gaines

Morgan
Tennessee

Confederate
Lookout
Station

PILINGS

Hartford

Metacomet   Tecumseh

FORT MORGAN

Manhattan

Port Royal
Richmond   Brooklyn

Octorara

Seminole   Winnebago
Lackawanna

Kennebec

Chickasaw

Monagahela

Itasca   Ossipee

Oneida   Galena

shrouds, just under the maintop, where the *Hartford*'s pilot, Martin Freeman, stood. What the admiral saw from this lofty station was awe inspiring. The long line of his ships was moving slowly down the channel behind him, clouds of smoke rolling from their gun ports as they hurled their salvos of shell and shrapnel. The guns of the fort thundered back with shot that sent sprays of smoking splinters shearing from the planking of the wooden vessels.

What Drayton, on the *Hartford*'s quarterdeck, saw as he peered up through the smoke high into the rigging made his heart flutter. There was his admiral, glass in one hand while gripping the rigging with the other, oblivious to the shot and shell, moving by degrees above the rising smoke. Here, in Drayton's eyes, was a disaster in the making. His worst nightmare visualized Farragut plunging suddenly from the rigging to the deck below or into the waters of the bay.

Soon the ship's signal quartermaster, on Drayton's orders, was climbing the rigging, a piece of line in one hand, scrambling after the admiral. Then, overriding Farragut's protest, the quartermaster passed the line around the admiral's body and made the ends fast in the shrouds. Farragut was lashed in the mizzen rigging and soon understanding the virtue of it. When he had to move up one more notch into the futtock rigging, he cast off the line but took it with him, lashing himself securely at his new perch.

Inside the *Tecumseh,* low in the water, Capt. T.A.M. Craven intently watched the *Tennessee.* His course was taking him west of the buoy at the end of the torpedo line, against Farragut's explicit orders. But the *Tennessee* was there, and the ram was Craven's responsibility. He steered his monitor straight for his prey—and right into the torpedo bed.

The sailors on the Confederate ram watched the slow-moving monitor steam toward them. Admiral Buchanan had ordered his gunners not to fire until the vessels were in actual contact. But Lt. A.D. Wharton's fingers drew the lockstring of

TUNIS AUGUSTUS MACDONOUGH CRAVEN

Tunis Augustus MacDonough Craven: born New Hampshire 1813; younger brother of Rear Adm. Thomas Tingey Craven; began navy career in 1829 as a midshipman after attending Columbia College; in 1835 began work on the U.S. Coastal Survey; lieutenant, 1841; served on the USS *Falmouth* and the USS *North Carolina* during the first half of the 1840s; in 1845 became chief editor of the *U.S. Nautical Magazine;* during the Mexican War served aboard the USS *Dale;* prior to the Civil War, commanded the steamer USS *Mohawk* and with it captured the slave ship *Wildfire* just off the coast of Cuba, freeing more than five hundred slaves; received special recognition from Queen Isabella II of Spain for rescuing the crew of a Spanish ship that had been wrecked on an island near Cuba; began his Civil War service at helm of the steamer USS *Crusader,* which he led into Key West to turn away Confederate forces and save the island for the Union; commanded USS *Tuscarora* and sailed across the Atlantic Ocean to search European waters for Confederate ships; after more than a year in this service, returned to America to take command of the ironclad USS *Tecumseh;* reinforced Adm. David Farragut's fleet on the evening of the battle of Mobile Bay; during the fighting, led the *Tecumseh* into action by firing the first shot; soon afterward the vessel hit a Confederate torpedo, which blasted a hole in the ironclad's hull, quickly sending the ship to the bottom. T.A.M. Craven was aboard the *Tecumseh* with most of its crew as it went under; only two officers and thirteen men escaped. In Craven's honor, the U.S. Navy later put his name on a destroyer.

the ram's bow gun tighter as he watched the Union ironclad draw nearer and nearer. Less than a hundred yards now separated them.

A torpedo exploded at 7:30 A.M. Engineer Harrie Webster aboard the monitor *Manhattan,* second in the line of ironclads, saw the *Tecumseh* lurch suddenly from side to side and careen violently over. The ironclad's stern lifted high in the air, and with its propeller spinning wildly, it pitched out of sight beneath the waves "like an arrow twanged from the bow." It had all happened in the blink of an eye.

Inside the stricken ironclad, there was little time for thought, let alone survival. Captain Craven and his pilot, Jean Collins, rushed instinctively for the narrow opening leading to safety, arriving at the same instant. Craven stepped back. "After you, pilot," he said. "There was nothing after me," Collins later reported, "for when I reached the top round of the ladder, the vessel seemed to drop from under me."

Inside the *Tennessee,* the Rebels, with their guns still trained on where the *Tecumseh* had been but an instant before, watched dumbfounded. Some broke into cheers, but many stared in awed silence, speaking together in low whispers. "They knew," Surgeon Conrad later wrote, "that the same fate was, probably, awaiting us, for we were then directly over the torpedo bed, and, shut up tightly as we were in our iron capsule, in another moment it might prove our coffin."

Aboard the *Hartford,* Farragut had also witnessed the sinking. He ordered Lt. Cmdr. James Edward Jouett, aboard the *Metacomet* lashed to the flagship's side, to put a boat in the water immediately to pick up survivors. Jouett did not need to be told to do this; he had already given the order. The little rescue boat, bobbing about in the boiling waters of the smoke-covered bay, was to find few alive—the *Tecumseh's* pilot, Jean Collins, and but twenty crew members. More than ninety men had gone down with Captain Craven. As the *Manhattan* steamed slowly over where the *Tecumseh* had been but a moment before, Harrie Webster thought of "the struggling wretches fighting with death" in the waters below.

In the *Brooklyn* at the head of the line of wooden warships, Capt. James Alden was stunned. "Assassination in its worst form!" he thought. "A glorious though terrible end for our noble friends, the intrepid pioneers of that death-strewed path! Immortal fame is theirs; peace to their names."

JAMES EDWARD JOUETT

James Edward Jouett: born Kentucky 1826; son of Matthew Harris (an artist) and Margaret Henderson (Allen) Jouett; midshipman, U.S. Navy, 1841; two years later served on the USS *Decatur* under Matthew C. Perry off the coast of Liberia in the so-called Berribee War; in 1847 campaigned aboard the USS *John Adams* off the east coast of Mexico and was present in the defense of Point Isabel; later shipped off on the USS *St. Lawrence* to the Mediterranean Sea; served aboard the USS *Lexington* and the USS *St. Mary's* in 1852; at the close of the decade, served as lieutenant on the USS *M.W. Chapin* during the Paraguay expedition; was captured by the Confederates while stationed at Pensacola when the Civil War began; provided a parole upon his release to never again take up arms against the Confederacy but soon aided in the closing of Galveston Harbor; led his famous charge by taking a party from the USS *Santee* and capturing the CSS *Royal Yacht,* the main ship that guarded the harbor entrance, on November 7–8, 1861; was wounded several times during the attack but showed his courage and skill by completing the capture

of the ship's crew and then setting the vessel afire; recognition of his actions at Galveston led to command of the USS *Montgomery* in late 1861 and then the USS *R.R. Cuyler* in April 1863; later appointed by Adm. David Farragut to command the fastest gunboat in his fleet, the USS *Metacomet;* during the battle of Mobile Bay, charged his ship into the bay with Farragut as the Federals took heavy fire; captured the CSS *Selma* during the fighting; later ran down many blockade runners; after the Civil War, took charge of the North Atlantic Squadron; rear admiral, 1884; subdued the Panama Canal revolt and restored peace to the area in 1885. James Jouett officially retired from the navy in 1890 and lived in Sandy Spring, Maryland, and Orlando, Florida, until his death in 1902.

But the *Tecumseh*'s violent end was only part of Alden's discomfort.

His ship was now entering the bay. But his lookouts reported shoal water just ahead of him, and as the smoke cleared for an instant, a row of suspicious looking buoys loomed directly under his bow. Alden stopped his engines.

On the *Hartford*, Farragut saw the *Brooklyn* stop and looked up anxiously at Martin Freeman in the foretop just above him in the rigging.

"What is the matter with the Brooklyn?" he asked anxiously. "Freeman, she must have plenty of water there."

"Plenty of water, and to spare, admiral," the pilot replied. Then he said, "but her screw is moving: I think she is going ahead again, sir."

But the *Brooklyn* was not going ahead. She was backing away and beginning to twist athwart the channel. Behind her the line of warships slowed.

The shouted question came from the flagship through a trumpet. "What's the trouble?"

"Torpedoes!" the *Brooklyn* answered.

If he swung around the *Brooklyn* past those buoys, Farragut knew he would find torpedoes there and possible disaster. He had earlier sent his flag lieutenant, J. Crittenden Watson, into the channel quietly and surreptitiously under the cover of night to reconnoiter the torpedo bed. There was no doubt that torpedoes were present. But refugees, deserters, and others had told Farragut that many of the devices had been so long in the water that they would probably not detonate.

With the *Brooklyn* now backing down on him, Farragut had to do something. His fleet could not just drift there, helpless and dead in the water, to be blasted to bits by the batteries of Fort Morgan. He had to take his chances.

"Damn the torpedoes!" he shouted. "Four bells! Captain Drayton, go ahead! Jouett, full speed!"

The *Hartford* slipped around the *Brooklyn* into the bed of torpedoes. Her crew heard the cones and kegs knocking against her bottom, their primers snapping. Any moment they could all be blown into oblivion.

As the flagship steamed into the lead, the *Brooklyn* stopped backing and followed. The rest of the fleet came after in line, as Farragut would later report, "their officers believing that they were going to a noble death with their commander in chief." He perhaps believed it himself.

But no more torpedoes exploded. Just before eight o'clock, the *Hartford* slipped into the unmined waters inside the bay, the paired ships of Farragut's fleet following. Only the *Oneida* in the rear of the line was having trouble. She was stricken, her boilers penetrated by a shot from the guns in the fort. But the *Galena*, a onetime experimental ironclad and now an unarmored screw sloop lashed to the *Oneida*, pulled and hauled. Running with the tide, the *Galena* tugged her crippled companion past the fort and, at about 8:30 A.M., into the torpedo-free waters of the bay. Farragut had done it. His fleet had successfully run the gauntlet of fire. It had survived the torpedoes and the fury of Fort Morgan.

But he was by no means out of trouble. Inside the bay, the great iron-beaked turtle that was the ram *Tennessee* moved like a monstrous avenger toward the *Hartford*. Farragut had expected this too. That was why he had positioned his ironclad monitors between himself and the ram. What he had not anticipated was the accurate fire now raking his ship from the three gunboats at the *Tennessee*'s side, killing sailors and doing unacceptable mischief on the open decks. At two minutes to eight o'clock, he cast off the *Metacomet*, which backed clear and immediately set off under full steam with orders to chase down and destroy or capture the Rebel gunboats.

Inside the *Tennessee*, Franklin Buchanan could not get his ponderous vessel into ramming position against the quicker *Hartford* and slid on by, merely exchanging booming shots with the Union flagship. Down the line the ram steamed at a sluggish two miles an hour, passing one ship after another as they entered the bay but unable to make contact. The ironclad could only flail at them with her powerful rifled guns, creating havoc but doing no serious damage. But neither could the wooden ships do the ram harm. Answering shots from the Federal men-of-war clanged and ricocheted uselessly off the ram's iron sides. The *Monongahela* rammed her in desperation, but the *Tennessee* simply shook her off.

As the paired ships entered the harbor, they quickly cast off from one another. Three of Farragut's gunboats—the *Port Royal*, the *Kennebec*, and the *Itasca*—immediately set off under full steam to help the *Metacomet* deal with the fleeing Rebel gunboats.

Two of the small Confederate vessels ran for their lives toward the protection of the fort, one of them, the *Gaines*, now mortally stricken. The *Metacomet*, with her greater speed, bore down mercilessly on the one gunboat unable to get away, the *Selma*.

Another irony was in the making. Thirty-eight-year-old Lt. Cmdr. James Jouett, captain of the *Metacomet*, had gone to college with Confederate lieutenant Peter U. Murphey, captain of the *Selma*. They had been classmates and close friends. For an hour, Jouett pursued his old friend in a running fight. A sudden passing rain squall swept the harbor, briefly hiding the pursued from the pursuer. But when the shower passed, the *Metacomet* had the *Selma* cornered.

In the Rebel gunboat, Murphey saw that the faster, more heavily armed *Metacomet* was about to rake his ship with grape and shrapnel and that the *Port Royal* was also about to open on him. Wounded in the left arm and bleeding, Murphey saw that further resistance was useless and struck his colors. Jouett accepted the surrender and, when it was done, smiled and pulled out a flask; the two former classmates drank to one another's health and to old and happier times.

Farragut had descended from the rigging when the *Hartford* passed the fort. Four miles inside the bay, he ordered his fleet to anchor with their hawse chains hove short for a quick weighing if necessary. The battle was not over by any means: other shots doubtless must yet be fired, more men perhaps had to die, for the *Tennessee* was still in the bay and unharmed. But Farragut's sailors had not had breakfast that

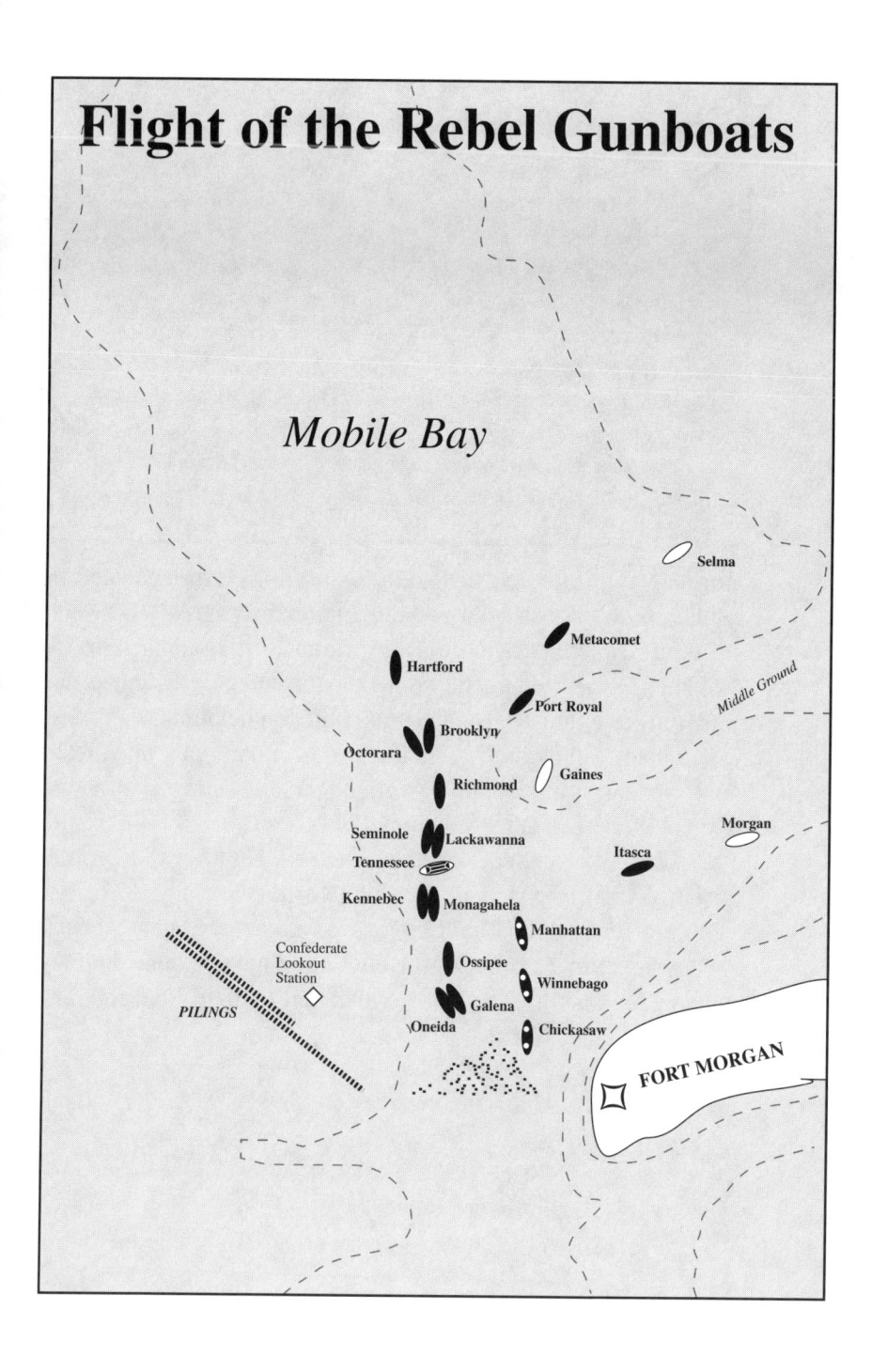

Flight of the Rebel Gunboats

Mobile Bay

Selma

Metacomet

Hartford

Port Royal

Middle Ground

Brooklyn

Octorara

Richmond

Gaines

Seminole

Lackawanna

Morgan

Tennessee

Itasca

Kennebec

Monagahela

Manhattan

Confederate
Lookout
Station

Ossipee

Winnebago

PILINGS

Galena

Oneida

Chickasaw

FORT MORGAN

PETER U. MURPHEY

Peter U. Murphey: born North Carolina 1810; midshipman, U.S. Navy, 1834; resigned his commission in April 1861 to join the Confederate navy as a first lieutenant; took command of the steamer CSS *Arrow* in Chesapeake Bay; served some time with the naval defenses of Virginia and North Carolina; transferred to Mobile Bay, Alabama, in 1862 to command the gunboat CSS *Morgan;* a few months later became commander of the gunboat CSS *Selma;* commanded the gunboat during the battle of Mobile Bay on August 5, 1864; received a wound in the arm during the fighting and lost his ship, captured by the Union fleet; taken to Pensacola Hospital for treatment; detained as a prisoner of war at Fort Warren, Boston, Massachusetts; exchanged and he returned to action for the Confederacy in October 1864; surrendered at the conclusion of the war and received his parole shortly afterward at Nanna Hubba Bluff, Alabama. Peter Murphey died on August 13, 1876, in Mobile, Alabama.

morning, and they had been through hellfire. They needed a respite, however brief it was likely to be.

As the *Hartford* lay still in the water, drifting at the end of its short anchor chain, Captain Drayton climbed to the poop deck to visit Farragut. He had something on his mind.

He said to the admiral, "What we have done has been well done, sir; but it all counts for nothing so long as the Tennessee is there under the guns of Morgan."

"I know it," replied Farragut, "and as soon as the people have had their breakfasts I am going for her."

In the *Tennessee* at about the same moment, Buchanan was saying something similar to the captain of his flagship. "Follow them up, Johnston," he said, "we can't let them off that way."

4
HELLFIRE IN THE HARBOR

In Mobile the bells were pealing. It had begun with the first deep-toned strokes of the guardhouse bell, ringing out in alarm, stroke rapidly following stroke. The big market bell began to ring, then the cathedral bell. In five minutes every bell in the city was pealing—"a pandemonium of sound," one young girl remembered, a "mad clanging of the bells."

News of the fighting had reached the city. Thousands began running for the shoreline to peer out into the harbor toward the fiery tableau in the distance. Their thought was not only for themselves but also for the men in the forts and on the Rebel ships, many of them friends or loved ones. Their hope at that moment was lodged with their sixty-three-year-old admiral and his dreaded ram.

Just as Farragut was the Federal navy's fort-running specialist, Franklin Buchanan was the Confederate navy's ironclad specialist. He had been in command of the very first ironclad in battle, the CSS *Virginia* (formerly the USS *Merrimac*), in March 1862 when it had attacked the Union's wooden fleet in Hampton Roads, Virginia; sunk the *Cumberland* and the *Congress*, two of the biggest Union ships of the line; and momentarily terrified the North.

But the price Buchanan had paid on that day of victory was a shot through the left thigh by a Federal minié ball fired from the shore. And on the next day, when the *Monitor*, the Union's own newly minted ironclad and the archetype of all subsequent Federal monitors, steamed into the scene and fought the epic standoff with the *Virginia*, Buchanan was sidelined.

Now, here in Mobile Bay, he was back in action, and the fight as usual was still in him.

Buchanan's friends, and even his enemies, called him Buck. He was of Scottish descent and slightly below middle height, compactly and powerfully built, with great physical strength, even at his age. He was eaglelike with a large Roman nose, which one of his officers described as "rather a 'hawk-bill.'" Befitting an admiral, he stood ramrod straight and walked much like a gamecock, although limping slightly now from the wound in his thigh. His forehead was high and fringed with snow-white hair, and he had steel-blue eyes. When full of fight, as he now was, he had a peculiarity of drawing down the corners of his mouth until the thin line between his lips formed a perfect arch around his chin.

Many believed that Buchanan and his ram, the CSS *Tennessee*, had been made for one another. They shared strong and striking similarities. One Union officer put it this way: "He, the last and only Confederate Admiral afloat—a stern, pitiless man, deaf to all considerations save those of mistaken duty to a bad cause, brave as a lion and a superb officer; it—their strongest, costliest and last ironclad, their boast and pride—they were indeed fitted to go down together."

But Buchanan also had his avuncular side. He had an affable and courteous nature and possessed great magnetism. He

FRANKLIN BUCHANAN

Franklin Buchanan: born Maryland 1800; entered the U.S. Navy in 1815 as a midshipman; after several years at sea promoted to lieutenant in 1825; promoted to commander in 1841; assisted Secretary of the Navy George Bancroft in the founding of the U.S. Naval Academy and in 1845 became its first superintendent; left the academy two years later to command the sloop USS *Germantown* during the Mexican War; later commanded Matthew C. Perry's flagship, USS *Susquehanna,* during the expedition to Japan, which opened that nation to U.S. trade and diplomatic relations; in 1855 promoted to captain and given command of the Washington Navy Yard; in 1861, after Massachusetts troops were fired upon in Baltimore, Buchanan assumed that Maryland would secede and tendered his resignation; later attempted to withdraw his resignation, but his request was denied; in August 1861 offered his services to the Confederacy; captain, C.S. Navy, September 1861; appointed to head the Office of Orders and Details; in February 1862 became flag officer in command of the James River defenses and the Chesapeake Bay Squadron with the newly completed ironclad CSS *Virginia* (formerly USS *Merrimac*) as flagship; attacked the Federal blockading fleet in Hampton Roads on March 8, 1862; after sinking the USS *Cumberland* and bombarding the USS *Congress* into submission, fire from Federal forces ashore interrupted the surrender process and Buchanan ordered the

frigate destroyed; Buchanan took up a rifle to participate in the destruction, but a Federal rifle ball struck his leg and disabled him; Lt. Catesby ap Roger Jones commanded the *Virginia* the following day in its famous battle with the Federal ironclad *Monitor;* full admiral and highest ranking officer, C.S. Navy, August 1862; in September assumed command of Mobile's defenses and worked diligently to improve them; during Federal admiral David G. Farragut's attack on August 5, 1864, most of Buchanan's fleet was quickly destroyed, leaving only his flagship, the recently completed ironclad CSS *Tennessee,* to face the enemy fleet; after a spirited battle in which Buchanan was again wounded, the *Tennessee* was surrounded and compelled to surrender; captured and imprisoned, Buchanan was not exchanged until March 1865; again assigned to Mobile, he did not reach the city before its capture by Federal forces in April and himself surrendered the next month. After the war he served briefly as president of Maryland Agricultural College and worked for a time as an insurance executive. Admiral Buchanan died at his Maryland home in 1874.

was enormously popular in Mobile, where he had been in command of the Rebel flotilla for two years since August 1862, when the city had become the most important Confederate port on the Gulf following the capture of New Orleans. The young belles of Mobile thought him a charming old gentleman, although he was, as one British observer noted sardonically, "at least ten years too young to be an admiral in England." Almost sixty-four, he was nearly a year older than his friend Farragut, with whom he had served in the U.S. Navy virtually since boyhood.

In the "old navy," Buchanan had been the first superintendent of the U.S. Naval Academy. He had commanded the USS *Susquehanna*, Commodore Matthew C. Perry's flagship, during its historic expedition to Japan in the 1850s. He was the Confederacy's senior admiral, and Farragut knew him well—in particular, how fearless he was.

It came as no surprise to the Federal commander, therefore, to see the *Tennessee* now steaming brazenly and alone straight for the Union armada.

Some of Buchanan's own men, however, were not just surprised but astonished. When he ordered Capt. James D. Johnston not to let the enemy off this way and turned and headed for the fleet, suppressed exclamations flew through the ship's crew: "The old admiral has not had his fight out yet," the sailors said, "he is heading for that big fleet; he will get his fill of it up there!"

His fleet surgeon, Daniel Conrad, could not believe it. "Are you going into that fleet, admiral?" he asked.

"I am, sir!" said Buchanan.

Without intending to be overheard, Conrad whispered to another officer standing nearby, "Well, we'll never come out of there whole!"

But Buchanan had overheard. Turning around he snapped at Conrad, "That's my lookout, sir!"

Buchanan knew he had six hours of coal aboard his ram

JAMES D. JOHNSTON

James D. Johnston: born Kentucky 1817; joined the U.S. Navy on June 30, 1832, as a midshipman; lieutenant, 1843; resigned his commission on April 10, 1861, to take up arms for the Confederacy; was a lighthouse inspector for the C.S. Navy at the beginning of the Civil War; commander of the ironclad CSS *Baltic* from 1861 to 1863; commander of the CSS *Tennessee*, 1864; most significant action was at Mobile Bay on August 5, 1864; fell wounded during the battle and forced to surrender his ship and sword by the U.S. Navy; released in October and returned to duty in the Mobile Bay area until the end of the war; in June 1865 traveled to Washington, D.C., securing his certificate of amnesty and proclaiming his intention of living in the Baltimore area; soon thereafter returned to Mobile to live near his brother and establish an insurance agency; in 1873 moved the business to Savannah, Georgia, where he lived until his death on May 9, 1896. Never having forgotten James Johnston's role in the battle of Mobile Bay, the son of Admiral Farragut offered to return the former Confederate sailor's sword as a friendly gesture in 1886.

and intended to burn it fighting. He did not mean to be trapped like a rat in a hole and made to surrender without a struggle.

The crew of the *Hartford* had just sat down to breakfast at about 8:45 A.M. when Farragut saw Buck coming. His urgent orders went out across the fleet: attack the *Tennessee*, not only with your guns, but ram her too, run her down at full speed.

Mess gear was hurriedly stowed and anchors weighed. Within minutes every ship in the flotilla was underway.

Aboard the *Tennessee*, as the first frigate sped toward her, Johnston passed the word: "Steady yourselves when she strikes. Stand by and be ready!"

The *Monongahela* struck her first, amidships on the starboard side, carrying away her own iron prow with the cutwater, without doing the ram much harm. As the *Monongahela*

The *Hartford* Engaging the *Tennessee*

slid away, firing a broadside as she passed, the *Lackawanna* hit the ram full on the port side at the after end of the casemate. Although the *Lackawanna*'s stem was cut and crushed to the plank ends from three feet above the waterline to five feet below, the only perceptible effect on the ram was to give her a momentary heavy list.

The *Lackawanna* rebounded and shuddered, then slid hard alongside the ram. Gazing down into the ports of the ironclad, the *Lackawanna*'s captain, J. B. Marchand, heard Rebel sailors using "most opprobrious language." The Federal marines on board, acutely offended by this Southern invective, opened fire with their muskets. A spittoon and a holystone were also hurled at the offending ports as the *Lackawanna* disengaged and wheeled into a turn for another approach.

The *Hartford* slammed next into the ram's port side, but it was only a glancing blow. As the two vessels grated past one another side by side, the *Hartford* fired a broadside pointblank into the ram with little effect. The *Tennessee*'s primers failed, so she was only able to get off one late answering shot, which penetrated the *Hartford*'s berth deck, wounding or killing several sailors.

Farragut again had the best seat in the house. When his flagship was about to ram the *Tennessee*, the admiral climbed into the port mizzen rigging this time, just above the deck. His flag lieutenant first remonstrated with him not to stand in such an exposed place, then, giving up, lashed him again to the rigging. As the *Hartford* struck the ironclad and slid past, Farragut was only a few feet above, staring down onto the decks of the hulking ship.

As the *Hartford* disengaged, the *Lackawanna* was just completing her long sweeping turn and charging in again. This time she rammed not the *Tennessee* but the *Hartford*, which had turned into her path, narrowly missing the admiral himself. After the collision, Farragut was in an instant climbing over the side to assess the damage. Immediately, a general outcry went up all around, "Get the Admiral out of the ship!"

The *Lackawanna* had struck the flagship just forward of the mizzenmast, crushing in her bulwarks, dismounting two guns, and slicing a jagged cut into her sides to within two feet of the waterline. The damage was substantial but not crippling.

When the *Lackawanna*, after that embarrassing interruption, had struck the ram a second blow and was making a turn for yet a third run, she once again came up breathtakingly close on the *Hartford*'s starboard side. She appeared ready to ram anything in her path, and the flagship seemed to have a penchant for being in her way.

Farragut turned to Lt. John Kinney, the signal officer from the Nineteenth Connecticut, who had been called above deck to help with ship-to-ship communications.

"Can you say, 'For God's sake' by signal?" Farragut demanded.

"Yes, sir," Kinney assured him.

"Then say to the *Lackawanna*, 'For God's sake get out of

our way and anchor!'"

In his haste to get this message to his counterpart on the *Lackawanna*, Kinney brought the butt-end of his signal flagstaff down hard on the admiral's head, causing him to duck and wince. The army signal officer on the *Lackawanna*, Lt. Myron Adams, who would one day be a minister taking God's messages, received the first five words of the admiral's dispatch, "For God's sake get out." At that point the wind in the foretop where Adams was perched caught the large U.S. flag at the *Lackawanna's* masthead and swirled it about him so that he completely missed the conclusion of the message. It did not seem to matter.

Inside the *Tennessee*, the fighting had turned into a living hell. The rammings had been bad enough, but now the ponderous Union ironclads had gotten in on the action. Buchanan's flagship was being mobbed by Farragut's fleet in this unequal contest. A Union officer recalled, "The whole fleet walked into her." The noise seemed to be one continuous deafening roar inside the ram. "It was the warmest place that I ever got into," one of the Rebel officers confessed.

The *Chickasaw* had succeeded in getting on the *Tennessee's* stern and was sticking there leechlike, never more than fifty yards distant, pounding away with her 11-inch guns. The ram's pilot, staring at the dogged monitor on his tail, turned to Johnston and said, "That d——d ironclad is hanging to us like a dog, and has smashed our shield already. Fight him! Sink him if you can!"

The rammings and the shots being poured into the *Tennessee* had set her plates jangling and bolts and splinters flying. Death was finding a way through the thick armor. The unrelenting bombardment had jammed the shutters on the ram's gun ports, and she could no longer fight back. Her last shot had been the misfire following the collision with the *Hartford*.

Buchanan was personally trying to get his guns back into

the fight when an iron splinter struck him in the leg just below the right knee, instantly breaking it. Summoned urgently to the scene, Dr. Conrad hoisted the old admiral on his back and began carrying him down the ladder to the cockpit below. Buchanan's limp broken leg slapped against the surgeon as he moved slowly along.

"Well, Johnston," Buchanan said to the ram's captain, "they have got me again. You'll have to look out for her now; it is your fight."

"All right," Johnston said, "I'll do the best I know how."

But Johnston knew there was not much fight left in his ship and that his best would not be good enough. Her smokestack had been shot away and smoke from the remaining stump was pouring in through the gratings into the gun deck, where the thermometer hovered at 120 degrees. The gun shutters were jammed and the ram's exposed steering chains had been shot away—she was drifting helplessly. As one eyewitness wrote, the *Tennessee* lay "like a bleeding stag at bay among the hounds."

Johnston again consulted Buchanan, and the admiral said simply, "Do the best you can, sir, and when all is done surrender."

The skipper saw around him nothing but impending disaster. It was now ten o'clock in the morning, and the hellish, one-sided fight had been raging for an hour. The *Chickasaw* was still hanging on the ram's stern, hammering away. The other monitors were doing their worst. The *Ossipee*, the next frigate in line for ramming, was approaching with throttle wide open. The *Monongahela*, the *Lackawanna*, and the *Hartford* were again bearing down. Johnston saw that his ram was nothing more now than a sitting target for the heavy guns of the frigates.

With "an almost bursting heart," he went on the deck of his battered ship and hoisted a white flag.

Ensign Charles E. Clark, commanding the guns on the bow

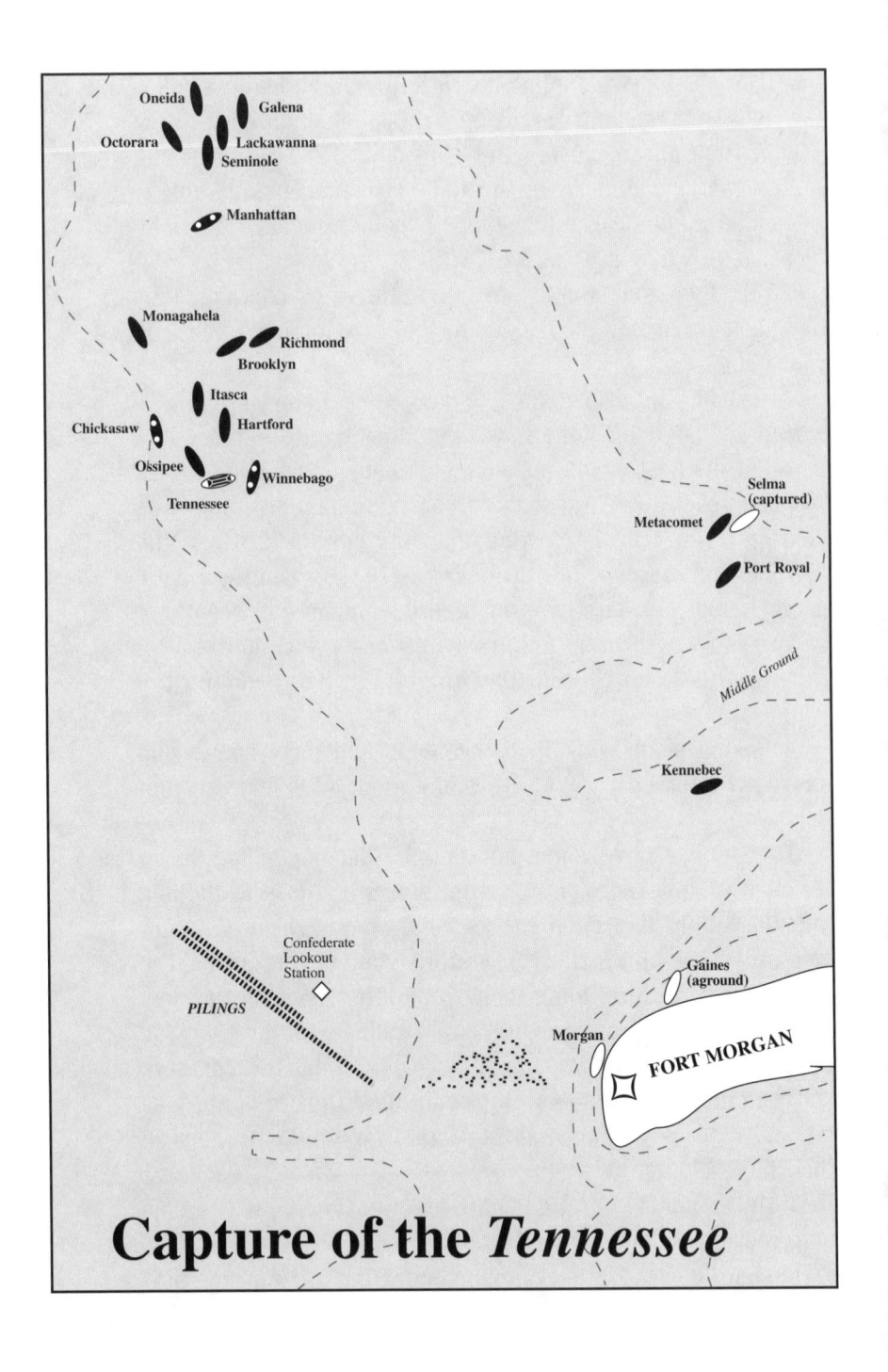

Capture of the *Tennessee*

Surrender of the *Tennessee*

of the *Ossipee*, saw Johnston suddenly appear above the casemate with the flag. Whirling about, he started aft on the dead run, shouting: "The ram has surrendered! She's showing a white flag!" The *Ossipee*'s captain, Cmdr. William E. Le Roy, had also seen the flag, nearly at the same instant. He began backing his ship's engines, putting his helm hard to starboard to avert the collision. It was too late. His ship hit the ram, but it was only a glancing blow.

As the ships came together, Le Roy appeared on the forecastle of his ship and shouted genially down to Johnston on the deck of the ram.

"Hallo, Johnston, old fellow! how are you? This is the United States Steamer *Ossipee*. I'll send a boat alongside for you. Le Roy, don't you know me?"

The Federal commander sent the promised boat, the U.S. flag was hoisted over the *Tennessee*, and the two old friends had the obligatory drink together.

Moments later, the *Chickasaw*, which had done the ram more damage than any other ship in the fleet, took the ironclad under tow and anchored her near the *Hartford;* Buchanan sent

WILLIAM EDGAR LE ROY

William Edgar Le Roy: born New York 1817; began his military career at fourteen as a midshipman in the U.S. Navy; lieutenant, July 1843; served on the flagship USS *Ohio* in the Mediterranean Sea; joined the crew of the steamer USS *Princeton* and took part in the engagement at Rio Aribiqua during the Mexican War; at the outbreak of the Civil War, promoted to commander and assigned to the steamer USS *Keystone State* of the South Atlantic Squadron; led the ship in action at Fernandina, Florida, in 1862; led an attack on ironclads near the shores of Charleston, South Carolina, a year later; during the battle of Mobile Bay, commanded the USS *Ossipee* and accepted the surrender of the ram CSS *Tennessee*; remained in the U.S. Navy after the war, captain, July 1866; commodore, 1870; rear admiral, April 1874; two years later commander of the South Atlantic Squadron; retired in March 1876. Four years later, William Le Roy died at the age of seventy-one. He would be remembered in the service by his nickname "the Chesterfield of the Navy."

his sword to his old friend Farragut but declined to see him. Captured with their admiral were about 190 officers and men aboard the *Tennessee* and another 90 on the *Selma*. The battle for Mobile Bay was over.

In hindsight, Farragut was to call it "a glorious victory" and his fight with the *Tennessee* in particular "one of the hardest earned victories of my life." One of his officers said, "We shall glory in this battle to our dying hour." But neither would they soon forget the cost—some 145 Union sailors and officers killed and 170 wounded.

But it was not yet a complete victory. There was still unfinished business onshore. Farragut began to see to it immediately, with a message to General Granger on Dauphin Island: "We have had our free fight with the forts."

The next move would be on land.

5
FALL OF THE FORTS

Maj. Gen. Gordon Granger already knew what had just happened in the bay and was calling it "a glorious day for our cause. The admiral, with his usual good luck and pluck, succeeded beyond all expectations, and in spite of all Fort Morgan and the rebel fleet could do." He understood the next job was his. And he had already begun.

Granger was an Indian-fighting ex-cavalryman, a West Pointer, reckless, handsome, ambitious, quick witted, warm blooded, and profane. He was a tall, partially bald, bewhiskered, forty-one-year-old New Yorker. And he was accustomed to beginning things on his own when the occasion demanded.

At the battle of Chickamauga the year before, when most of the Union army under Maj. Gen. William Rosecrans was retreating in disorder, Granger, without orders, had marched against the flow into what was left of the fight. Leaving the

GORDON GRANGER

Gordon Granger: born New York 1822; graduated West Point in 1845; second lieutenant, 2d Infantry, 1845; transferred to the Regiment of Mounted Riflemen (later the 3d Cavalry); active during the Mexican War with General Scott's army at Veracruz, Cerro Gordo, Contreras, Churubusco, Chapultepec, and the siege of the city of Mexico; first lieutenant, 1852; captain, 1861; brevetted for gallant conduct at the battle of Wilson's Creek; colonel, 2d Michigan Calvary, 1861; took part in operations against New Madrid, Island No. 10, and the advance against and siege of Corinth; brigadier general, U.S. Volunteers, 1862; participated with the Army of Kentucky and the Army of Tennessee; major general, U.S. Volunteers, 1862; helped repel Maj. Gen. Nathan Bedford Forrest's Tennessee raid of June 1863; with Maj. Gen. William Rosecrans's army at Chickamauga, his decisive use of the Reserve Corps supported Maj. Gen. George Thomas's position, winning him the utmost praise from Generals G. W. Cullum and T. J. Wood; commanded the Fourth Corps at Chattanooga, including the battle of Missionary Ridge; captured Forts Gaines and Morgan by land in August 1864; helped capture the city of Mobile in April 1865; mustered out of the volunteer service in January 1866; colonel, 25th U.S. Infantry, 1866; at the age of forty-seven married Maria Letcher of Lexington, Kentucky. While in command of the District of New Mexico, Gordon Granger died in Santa Fe on January 10, 1846.

pass he was guarding several miles in the rear, he had hurried forward with all of his available troops. Attacking furiously with two brigades, he then drove back the Confederates on the right as they closed around Maj. Gen. George Thomas, who with an ad hoc command was standing like a rock, trying to redeem the day. It was Granger and Thomas who had prevented a Union defeat from becoming a total rout.

Granger was outspoken and rough edged in manner but kindly and sympathetic at heart. His independence occasionally bordered on insubordination, and at times he lacked energy; he seemed to be at his best only in emergencies. The general was, as Rosecrans said, "great in battle."

CHARLES DEWITT ANDERSON

Charles DeWitt Anderson: born South Carolina 1827; sailed with family to Texas in 1836 and was orphaned upon his arrival; reared by a local Episcopal minister; attended the U.S. Military Academy but left West Point after his freshman year; in 1856 commissioned from civilian life to lieutenant of artillery, U.S. Army; served with the 4th Artillery in Florida and Utah; upon the outbreak of Civil War, returned to the South and entered Confederate service as a captain; took command of ordnance duties at Fort Morgan, an earthen fortification that was part of the outer defenses of Mobile Bay; later briefly served as major of the 20th Alabama Infantry and on the staff of Brig. Gen. Adley H. Gladden—at Shiloh, Gladden was killed and his staff dissolved afterward; returned to Mobile; colonel, 21st Alabama, May 1862; in command of Fort Gaines on Dauphin Island, across the bay from Fort Morgan, 1862; after Adm. David Farragut's fleet ran past the forts, Federal troops landed on Dauphin Island, and soon after Anderson surrendered Fort Gaines; passed the remainder of the war in a New Orleans prison; after his release moved to Texas to work on railroad construction; later served as Austin's city engineer and built the Galveston lighthouse; remained as the lighthouse's operator until his death in November 1901. Colonel Anderson is remembered for his surrender of Fort Gaines, which was criticized as an act of cowardice by many Confederates, but numerous Federal authorities, including Admiral Farragut, acknowledged his bravery in holding the position so gallantly for as long as he did.

The situation before Forts Gaines and Morgan looked like an emergency to Granger, and he had been working with energy since landing on Dauphin Island on August 3. By midnight on the fourth, he had his light artillery in position within twelve hundred yards of Fort Gaines and had opened on the works in consort with the Union fleet's passage into the bay.

Even as the *Tennessee* was surrendering in the harbor, Granger was debarking his heavy guns on the south side of the island near Pelican Island Spit. Placing the guns in the deep sand was hard, slow going. Everything had to be hauled and packed on the men's backs, and the sand was hot enough during the day "for roasting potatoes." But Granger had the artillery in position to open on the fort by daylight the next day, Saturday, August 6. Fort Gaines found itself cut off and under siege, not only by Granger but also by the guns of Farragut's fleet.

RICHARD LUCIAN PAGE

Richard Lucian Page: born Virginia 1807; cousin of Robert E. Lee; enlisted in the U.S. Navy in 1824; lieutenant, 1836; commander, 1855; served with the Pacific Squadron during the Mexican War; upon his return to the United States, worked as assistant inspector of ordnance at Norfolk, Virginia, naval yard; joined the Virginia State Navy when the Civil War began and helped plan the defenses of the James River; in June 1862 joined the Confederate navy as a commander and again appointed ordnance officer at Norfolk; soon promoted to captain, participated at the battle of Port Royal, South Carolina; organized the evacuation of Norfolk's naval operations to Charlotte, North Carolina, establishing a major Confederate depot there; in command at Charlotte until 1864; transferred to the army and commissioned brigadier general in March 1864; placed in command of the defenses of Mobile Bay; headquartered at Fort Morgan, in August 1864 he was forced to surrender the post to Federal forces after Adm. David Farragut's fleet successfully ran the gauntlet of mines in the bay and cut off the fort's supply lines; imprisoned until July 1865; after the war, returned to Norfolk and became a businessman; served as superintendent of schools from 1875 to 1883. Richard Page died in August 1901 at Blue Ridge Summit, Pennsylvania.

The situation was becoming too much for Col. Charles D. Anderson of the 21st Alabama, commanding the fort. From where he was sitting, it appeared impossible for him to maintain his position in the face of all that firepower. He had hoped to hold out longer, but confronted by a likely mutiny of his men, who had petitioned him to surrender, he ran up a flag of truce and requested a meeting with the enemy.

When Brig. Gen. Richard L. Page, Anderson's immediate superior at Fort Morgan, heard of this on August 7, he frantically began trying to prevent capitulation. Page signaled Anderson demanding an explanation. The demand went unacknowledged, even though Page fired guns to get Anderson's attention and telegraphed repeatedly in case the colonel was on the lookout but unable to signal. "Hold on to your fort" was Page's cryptic order. Hearing nothing back, Page went to Fort Gaines in person that night under cover of darkness only to find Anderson absent in the fleet, talking surrender. Page left peremptory orders that any terms his subordinate might make with the enemy were to be revoked and that he was relieved of command. The next morning, Page fired signal guns from Fort Morgan and telegraphed with the same message.

But the terms were by then agreed to. The die was cast. At 9:30 in the morning, Monday, August 8, Anderson surrendered, and the Union flag was hoisted over Fort Gaines to the cheers of Farragut's seamen. More than eight hundred officers and men were taken prisoner, and twenty-six guns and a large supply of ordnance and subsistence stores were seized. Page fumed, calling Anderson's conduct "inexplicable and disgraceful."

If Page had been unable to get Anderson's attention, he was now about to get Granger's and Farragut's. A summons was sent immediately to Fort Morgan from the Union general and admiral to surrender or suffer the consequences. Page replied with defiance: "I am prepared to sacrifice life and will only surrender when I have no means of defense."

Page was like that. Farragut also knew him well. The Confederate brigadier was a rare hybrid, a man who had been a commander in the U.S. Navy before the war and was now a captain in the Confederate navy. He had only received his commission and rank in the army as well when he had been put in command of the outer defenses of Mobile Bay in March. He was fifty-eight years old, tall and erect, with the air of a man who had seen service and was accustomed to command. He was a cousin of Confederate general Robert E. Lee, and like his cousin, whom he resembled physically, he was quiet and gentlemanly, but he was also a vigorous disciplinarian. In the "old navy" he was known as "Ramrod" Page.

With the Rebel commander's defiant words of rejection in hand, Granger sent a request to New Orleans for an additional three thousand men and moved without delay to Mobile Point, near Pilot Town, to invest Fort Morgan. Farragut, ever cooperative, sent his monitors with orders to alternate shelling into the fort every fifteen or twenty minutes day and night—to "amuse" the garrison.

On the evening of August 21, Granger told Farragut that his batteries would be ready to open on Fort Morgan in earnest at daylight the next morning. The admiral ordered his fleet to move into position to open fire on the fort at long range simultaneously.

The bombardment began at daylight. All day Fort Morgan was hammered by batteries on land and by the ships in the bay. At 8:30 that night, the citadel in the fort caught fire and Granger ordered his near batteries to redouble their pounding. At six o'clock in the morning, August 23, an explosion rocked the fort, and half an hour later Page concluded he no longer had the means of defense.

The trenches of the enemy had reached the glacis in front of the fort, the walls were breached, and all his guns save two were disabled. The fires that had consumed the citadel were now threatening the magazines. Page ordered all of his powder destroyed, every gun spiked or otherwise damaged, and everything that could possibly be of use to the Federals wrecked. With his fort now a mass of debris, he ran up the white flag.

Farragut immediately sent Drayton to meet Granger to arrange surrender terms. At two o'clock in the afternoon, Page surrendered the fort, its garrison of about six hundred men, and its sixty pieces of useless artillery. The Union flag was hoisted over its ramparts to a one-hundred-gun salute from the Federal fleet.

The bay was theirs, the three forts were theirs—little Fort Powell had been abandoned and blown up the night of August 5. The stage was now set to do something about the city of Mobile itself—if the North could just figure out what.

But Mobile was a different problem entirely, a nut at this

point far too hard to crack. Maj. Gen. Edward R.S. Canby, in overall command of Federal land forces in the Gulf and Granger's boss, directed from New Orleans: "No direct attack will be made upon Mobile until we have a larger land force than can [now] be spared."

Farragut could only grudgingly agree. "If I did not think Mobile would be an elephant to hold," he said, "I would send up the light-draft ironclads and try that city, but I fear we are not in a condition to hold it." He would have to content himself with what he did have—"quite a colony here now—two forts, a big fleet, and a bay to run about in."

The Confederates did not find this amusing. Mary Chesnut, the South Carolina diarist, wrote unhappily in a series of entries in August: "Misery upon misery. Mobile going as New Orleans went. . . . Mobile stripped for the fight—noncombatants ordered out of the town. Horrid times ahead. . . . Mobile half-taken."

Confederate major general Dabney Herndon Maury, commanding Rebel forces in Mobile, had basically the same unhappy take on the situation. With Fort Morgan gone, Maury was expecting an attack on the city at once. Even before then, he had been preparing for the worst. "Have the engineers do all possible to strengthen the forts of the inner harbor line and city defenses," he had ordered his commanders on August 8. That same day he wired Confederate secretary of war John Seddon in Richmond: "Forts Powell and Gaines surrendered. Can you spare any good infantry?"

Four days later Maury told Seddon, "Henceforth I must collect and hold here everything necessary for a beleaguered city." He had six months' supply of food on hand for a garrison. Ordnance supplies, however, were insufficient to withstand a siege. But what he was most worried about were the civilians in Mobile. The city had probably more women and children in it than at any time since the war began.

Maury was in for it—all of Mobile was. It seemed now just a matter of time.

6
MARCH OF THE YANKEE COLUMNS

It was once said of Dabney Maury that he was the perfect type of old-time Virginia army officer. His obituary, written many years later, described him as "brave, high-spirited, adventurous, rollicking, always ready for fighting, ready for sport in any form, ready for any undertaking that offered adventure, or if honor and duty required, ready to sacrifice life for either."

His view of himself was that there had been improvement over time. "'In regard of liquor,'" he had written a friend before the war, "I do not get tight quite so often."

Maury's pedigree was impressive. He was the son of Capt. John Minor Maury of the U.S. Navy. When his father died of yellow fever while fighting pirates in 1828, little Dabney fell

DABNEY HERNDON MAURY

Dabney Herndon Maury: born Virginia 1822; graduated from the University of Virginia in 1842 and then attended the U.S. Military Academy, graduating thirty-seventh of fifty-nine in the class of 1846; brevetted second lieutenant and assigned to the Regiment of Mounted Rifles; fought in the Mexican War, wounded in the arm at Cerro Gordo, and brevetted first lieutenant; afterward returned to West Point to teach; was stationed on the Texas frontier at the outbreak of Civil War; joined the Confederate army; captain, cavalry, June 1861; colonel, February 1862; chief of staff for Maj. Gen. Earl Van Dorn at Pea Ridge; brigadier general, March 1862; fought well while leading a division at the battle of Corinth in October 1862; major general, November 1862; sent to Vicksburg in December and gave good service during the early defense of that post; named commander of the Department of East Tennessee in April 1863; in May became commander of the District of the Gulf, headquartered at Mobile; dutifully defended the city with all his energy and limited resources, but in April 1865, overwhelmed by superior Federal forces, had to evacuate; surrendered the following month as part  of Lt. Gen. Richard Taylor's command; after the war, founded and taught at a boy's school in Fredericksburg, Virginia; in 1868 organized the Southern Historical Society and served as executive chair until 1886; served as U.S. minister to Columbia from 1885 to 1889; upon his return to the United States, lived with his son in Peoria, Illinois, until his death in January 1900. Dabney Maury is best described as a fine Virginia gentlemen who served honorably as a productive soldier, writer, teacher, and civil servant.

under the care of a guardian, his uncle Matthew Fontaine Maury, who was celebrated worldwide for his work in mapping the oceans. Dabney had a frank smile and a high cheery voice that could penetrate to the distant corners of a building, ship, fortress, or battlefield.

He had a heart filled with good fellowship and an outsized soul full of duty, honor, and honesty. But all this largeness of heart and soul was encased in a body entirely too small. He was "every inch a soldier," one of his cannoneers said, "but then there were not many inches of him." He was only five feet, three inches tall on a very tall day, and his soldiers called him "Puss in Boots," for half of his diminutive person seemed hopelessly lost in the pair of enormous hip-high cavalry boots he wore.

At West Point, when his section was studying the construction of fortifications, Prof. Dennis Hart Mahan asked, "Mr. Maury, what is the height of the breast-height slope?"

"Five feet, sir," the cadet replied.

Mahan, celebrated for his terrorizing sarcasm, regarded the diminutive Virginian with a cold eye and said, "If it were five feet, Mr. Maury, you could not shoot over it."

Maury graduated from West Point in 1846 as a member of the class generally considered the most star filled of the antebellum years. He had prided himself in being always in the inconspicuous middle of its conspicuous lineup, in what he called "that easiest and safest of positions." He had graduated thirty-seventh in a class of fifty-nine, maintaining his place near the middle with a spurt when necessary—he had always been good at a spurt. And one spurt he had been particularly good at so far had been the Civil War, in which he had demonstrated conspicuous competence in every command he had held in the Confederate army.

As Maj. Gen. Earl Van Dorn's chief of staff in the Trans-Mississippi West in 1862, he had proved invaluable in both preparing for battle and waging it. He had distinguished himself at Pea Ridge in Arkansas. "Here, as on other battle-fields where I have served with him," Van Dorn wrote, "he proved to be a zealous patriot and true soldier; cool and calm under all circumstances, he was always ready, either with his sword or his pen."

Now forty-two years old, Maury had been in command of Confederate forces in the Gulf District, with headquarters at Mobile, since May 1863. His immediate superior, Lt. Gen.

Richard Taylor, found Maury to be a great comfort. He was in Taylor's view an able officer "who not only adopted my plans, but improved and executed them."

Six uneasy months after the battle of Mobile Bay, the attack Maury expected any moment had not yet come. Farragut had gone on to other things, and it had taken the Union army time to marshal the necessary forces. But by February 1865 the time was at hand, and the Federals knew Maury would not be an easy conquest. The Union army's general in chief, Ulysses S. Grant, had it on good authority that the Confederate commander at Mobile was under orders to hold out to the last.

Maury had about nine thousand troops with three hundred field and siege guns, four gunboats, two remaining big forts— Spanish and Blakely—and his bristling three lines of defense. His little army was made up mostly of odds and ends and hand-me-downs, fragments of other commands that had already given out by this twilight of the Confederacy. But these remnants, other than a callow boy militia he also had, were seasoned fighters, many of them battle-hardened veterans from Gen. John B. Hood's battered and beaten Army of Tennessee.

The job of prying Maury out of Mobile had fallen to Union major general E.R.S. Canby, as tall and taciturn as Maury was short and sociable. Canby was Kentucky-born (though reared in Indiana), forty-eight years old, clean shaven, mild mannered, soldierly looking, and wooden. He was patient, courteous, and reserved; calm, precise, placid, puritanical, and a little dry; but he was also kindly and easy in conversation when one got to know him.

Canby had had very little field experience in the war, but he had driven the Confederate invaders from New Mexico Territory in 1862 and had commanded the Federal troops during the New York City draft riots in the summer of 1863. He was known to be brave, just, and conscientious and was generally esteemed by all who knew him. Considered an able

EDWARD RICHARD SPRIGG CANBY

Edward Richard Sprigg Canby: born Kentucky 1817; began military career in 1835 when appointed a cadet at West Point; graduated four years later; second lieutenant, 2d Infantry, 1839; first lieutenant, 1846; captain and adjutant general, 1847; participated with General Scott's army in the attack on Veracruz and the battles of Cerro Gordo, Contreras, Churubusco; took part in the capture of Mexico City; afterward worked in California on staff duty; major, 10th Infantry, 1855; stationed at Fort Defiance in New Mexico Territory at outbreak of Civil War; colonel, 19th Infantry, and commander of the Department of New Mexico, 1861; played crucial role by stopping Brig. Gen. Henry H. Sibley's invasion of New Mexico—a push the Confederacy hoped would lead to the capture of the gold-fields of the West to finance their war effort; brigadier general, U.S. Volunteers,1862; transferred east to work in Washington and New York City; major general, U.S. Volunteers, 1864; took command of the Military Division of West Mississippi and remained there until late 1864; led ground campaign against Mobile and captured the city on April 12, 1865; a month later received the surrender papers of the last two Confederate armies in the field, commanded by Richard Taylor and Edmund Kirby Smith; brigadier general, U.S. Army,1866; assigned command of the Department of Columbia and then the Division of the Pacific. General Canby was attacked and killed by Captain Jack and other Modoc Indians during negotiations on their removal from the Lava Beds of Siskiyou County, California, on April 11, 1873.

administrator, nobody mistook him for a Grant, a Sherman, a Sheridan, or any other great field commander. At West Point he had finished next to last in his class in 1839 and was what one officer described as "a strong instance of the faithful cultivation of rather mediocre gifts."

But his command was the largest geographically in the Union army, stretching from the Florida Peninsula to the mouth of the Rio Grande, a territory that embraced Florida, Alabama, Mississippi, Louisiana, Texas, Arkansas, and Missouri. And Mobile was by March 1865 his primary target.

In the antebellum army Canby and Maury had been friends and fellow officers. When the Civil War began, Maury was the adjutant for the Department of New Mexico in Santa Fe, where the Canbys, new arrivals, had been staying temporarily with the Maurys. When the news of the attack on Fort Sumter arrived, Maury had resigned and prepared to return home to fight for his state of Virginia. But ever the considerate Southerner, he had waited first for the return of Canby, who was out leading a large expedition against the Navajos. When his friend returned hot and dusty from the chase, Maury carefully explained to him how and where he had distributed the troops in the department. He had then turned both his office and his house over to Canby and left for Fort Leavenworth and from there to Richmond.

Maury and Canby had not seen one another since that spring of 1861. Now it was the spring of 1865, and here was Canby again, only with 45,000 armed troops this time, still wanting both Maury's house and his command. Some things, it seems, never change.

Canby's plan was to advance on Mobile in two columns from the east. The main column, 32,000 men under Canby's personal command, would move on the city from Fort Morgan and lay siege to Spanish Fort. The second column, 13,000 troops under Maj. Gen. Frederick Steele, would march in a series of feinting movements toward Mobile from Pensacola and invest Fort Blakely. The warships of the West Gulf Blockading Squadron, now under the command of Adm. Henry K. Thatcher, would support the movement from the waters of the bay. The idea was to overrun the two forts, turn the strong defenses at Mobile, and force the city's surrender or evacuation.

To do this work, Canby had two army corps—the Thirteenth, under Gordon Granger, and the Sixteenth, under Maj. Gen. Andrew Jackson Smith—plus all of the necessary adjuncts: a colored division, cavalry brigade, engineering brigade, and siege train.

Frederick Steele

Frederick Steele: born New York 1819; graduated from the U.S. Military Academy in 1843, thirtieth in his class of thirty-nine that included U. S. Grant; commissioned second lieutenant and posted to infantry; after performing routine frontier and garrison duty, served with distinction in the Mexican War, winning brevets to first lieutenant and captain and promotion to first lieutenant; captain, 1855; major, 11th infantry, 1861; in the opening stages of the Civil War, he commanded U.S. regulars at the battle of Wilson's Creek, Missouri; moving to the volunteer organization, he was named colonel of the 8th Iowa Infantry in September 1861; brigadier general, U.S. Volunteers, January 1862; commanded the District of Southeast Missouri; led a division in the capture of Helena, Arkansas, and in Maj. Gen. W. T. Sherman's repulse at Chickasaw Bluffs; major general, U.S. Volunteers, March 1863; commanded a division in the Army of the Tennessee during the Vicksburg campaign of 1863; placed in command of the Department of Arkansas; directed the Arkansas portion of the Red River campaign in the spring of 1864 and after taking Camden was driven back to Little Rock with heavy losses; in 1865 led a division in Maj. Gen. E.R.S. Canby's campaign against Mobile; brevetted through major general, U.S. Army, was finally mustered out of the volunteer service in 1867; continued in the regular army as colonel of the 20th Infantry. In 1868, while on leave in California, Steele suffered an attack of apoplexy and fell from a carriage. He died shortly thereafter.

Smith's corps was Canby's newest acquisition. Smith, like Granger, was an old Indian fighter. He was nearly fifty now, bluff, brusque, stirring, grizzled, and choleric, and had been almost everywhere. If there was a general utility unit in the Union army, it was Smith's command, called in throughout the war to go where most needed. So often had Smith been shipped out to some new command for some new emergency that he called his troops "the Wandering Tribe of Israel."

"Like a Viking," one officer described him, "he voyaged

ANDREW JACKSON SMITH

Andrew Jackson Smith: born Pennsylvania 1815; graduated U.S. Military Academy in 1838, thirty-sixth in his class of forty-five; commissioned second lieutenant and posted to 1st Dragoons; saw service on the western frontier and in the Mexican War; first lieutenant 1845; captain 1847; major 1861; colonel and chief of cavalry to Maj. Gen. Henry Halleck during his advance on Corinth, Mississippi, 1862; brigadier general, U.S. Volunteers, 1862; commanded a division in Maj. Gen. William T. Sherman's attack on Chickasaw Bluffs and throughout the Vicksburg campaign of 1863; detached to support Maj. Gen. Nathaniel P. Banks's Red River campaign in the spring of 1864; defeated Confederates at Pleasant Hill, Louisiana, but was angered by the campaign's overall failure and Banks's ineffectiveness; major general, U.S. Volunteers, 1864, won an independent action at Tupelo, Mississippi, while still detached before moving into Missouri and finally Tennessee; joined Maj. Gen. George Thomas's command in the rout of Gen. John B. Hood's forces at Nashville in December 1864; led the Sixteenth Corps in the operations against Mobile 1865; brevetted brigadier general, U.S. Army, for Pleasant Hill and major general for Nashville; continuing in the service after the war, became colonel of the 7th U.S. Cavalry; resigned his commission in 1869; in civil service in St. Louis; placed on the retired list in 1889 by the army with the rank of colonel of cavalry; died at St. Louis in 1897. Although not as recognized as many of his contemporaries, General Smith was nonetheless one of the most capable officers to serve the Union. He proved equally effective in a subordinate role or in independent action. His soldiers were among the hardest marchers and toughest fighters on either side during the war.

through the country, descending from his boats and taking a hand in any fight where he happened to be." Smith had been prominent at Corinth, Arkansas Bluffs, Jackson, Vicksburg, the Red River campaign, in Mississippi in the sorties to find and fight the elusive cavalry of Confederate major general Nathan Bedford Forrest, and most recently in the Union victory at Nashville. When detached from Nashville and sent to the Gulf in early February, Smith's wandering tribe did not even have a corps number or a name. When it arrived in the land of Canby, it became the Sixteenth Corps, assuming an old deactivated designation reactivated for the occasion.

The rainy season usually ended in southern Alabama during the first ten days of March. It had lingered a little longer this year, and Canby had been delayed by rain and windstorms. As he had waited for the skies to clear, the Union high command had become ever more impatient. But finally the weather lifted, and Canby began his move toward Spanish Fort on March 17. Two days later, Steele, a seasoned forty-six-year-old infantryman from Delaware, left Pensacola. It all began under the most seemingly favorable conditions, the skies clear, the weather beautiful, the roads dry.

Early into the march, however, the weather closed in again. Rain began to fall, and Canby's army was suddenly being lashed by a vicious deluge of biblical proportions. The rain poured down, overflowing rivers, sweeping away bridges, and turning the entire region into a vast quagmire. Wagons sank to their axles while standing in park, and animals foundered, unable to move. Horses, wagons, and artillery caissons had to be hauled by hundreds of shouting, cursing troops buried to their knees in mud.

Steele's command, trying to make the one hundred miles from Pensacola to Blakely, had to march through swamps and quicksand and was obliged to corduroy and bridge fifty miles of road along the way. Canby said the storms bogging down his army had not been paralleled "in the last forty years."

Maury's little force of defenders watched as the Union army slogged toward them, slashing at its flanks with small cavalry charges, looking for opportunities to separate the slowly advancing columns so they might be attacked in detail.

Maury's troops were but swarming bees tormenting a lumbering bear and nothing more. It was obvious to the Confederates what would happen when the weather lifted. The Union juggernaut was coming and there was little that could be done to stop it. "I now think there can be no longer any doubt upon the subject," Confederate brigadier general St. John R. Liddell wrote Maury on March 22 from Fort Blakely. "It is sad to think of the desolation that will follow the traces of these devastating columns of Yankees. . . . I don't think we will be permitted to remain in quiet long."

Maury had hoped to whip Canby's superior force in detail in open fights during their approach. As this now seemed out of the question, he pulled back his forces into the two forts and waited for the enemy to come to him.

From the beginning, Maury had harbored no illusions. He considered the campaign bootless, begun when "scarce a hope was left of that independence for which we had fought four years." Union forces would soon turn Robert E. Lee's flank at Petersburg, followed by the subsequent race to Appomattox and surrender. The end of the Confederacy was at hand and everybody knew it. It was senseless to believe that Maury in Mobile with his 9,000 men against Canby's 45,000 could redeem a lost war. He could only hold out as long as possible without risking the ultimate safety of his command and then cut and run. Those, in fact, were his orders from General Taylor. But first the Virginian intended to put up a respectable parting fight.

It was not until March 24 that the skies lifted and the Union columns got well under way again. Three days later, on the twenty-seventh, Canby drew up before Spanish Fort and put it under siege.

7

SHOWDOWN AT SPANISH FORT

Maury's two outer ramparts, Spanish Fort and Fort Blakely, were five miles apart, separated by marshes and bayous, a yawning no-man's-land considered impractical for military operations, offensive or defensive. And they were commanded by two men just as far apart in style and substance.

In overall command of these bastions was Brig. Gen. St. John R. Liddell, a forty-nine-year-old Mississippian with the personality of a porcupine. He was contentious, hard to get along with, and known to detest his superiors. Since he was blunt and honest, he never moderated his views to suit anyone above or below him and had therefore often been in trouble. But he liked Maury, whom he considered "a good man, kind and generous. . . . My position and social relations with him were very pleasant."

When Liddell reported to Mobile in the late summer of 1864, Maury assigned him to command of the city's two east-

ST. JOHN RICHARDSON LIDDELL

St. John Richardson Liddell: born Mississippi 1815; attended the U.S. Military Academy in 1833 but was discharged for academic reasons after his freshman year; lived and worked at his father's plantation in Catahoula Parish, Louisiana, until the outbreak of Civil War; began Confederate service as a colonel on Maj. Gen. William J. Hardee's staff, in February 1862 carrying messages to Richmond for Gen. Albert Sidney Johnston; at the siege of Corinth commanded an Arkansas brigade; brigadier general, July 1862; fought at Perryville during the Kentucky campaign and participated at Murfreesboro, Chickamauga, and Chattanooga; in December 1863, by his own request, transferred to the Trans-Mississippi Department; during the Red River campaign assisted in repulsing Maj. Gen. Nathaniel P. Bank's Federal forces advancing toward Shreveport, Louisiana; in July 1864 commanded the District of the Gulf, which included the eastern half of Mobile Bay; helped defend Spanish Fort until it's evacuation in early April 1865; captured with the garrison of Fort Blakely later that month; after the war returned to his Louisiana plantation, where a bitter feud erupted with his neighbor Charles Jones. The dispute and St. John Liddell's life came to tragic end in February 1870 when Liddell was shot and killed on a steamboat in the Black River by Jones and his sons.

ern forts, and he had headquartered at Blakely.

Liddell's lieutenant at Spanish Fort was Brig. Gen. Randall Lee Gibson, a thirty-three-year-old lawyer and sugar planter from Louisiana. He had graduated from Yale College in 1853 and from the University of Louisiana Law Department in 1855. He had fought in the Atlanta and Nashville campaigns before coming to Mobile. A bachelor, Gibson was a man of extensive learning, a ready debater, logical and accurate in his speech, aristocratic in bearing, always courteous and gentle, companionable, and entertaining.

Looking out now on the mighty host of Yankees gathering before his ancient fort, Gibson had digging on his mind. "You must dig, dig, dig," he told his soldiers. "Nothing can save us here but the spade."

The Confederate line of defense at Spanish Fort ran about 2,500 yards in an arc, its right flank resting on the Apalachee River and its left on Bayou Minette. At its back was the torpe-

RANDALL LEE GIBSON

Randall Lee Gibson: born Kentucky 1832; grew up at his parent's plantation in Terrebonne Parish, Louisiana; after graduating from Yale, attended law school at the University of Louisiana and graduated in 1855; traveled throughout Europe afterward and served briefly as military attaché with the U.S. Embassy in Spain; returned to the United States in 1858 and established his own sugar plantation in southern Louisiana; at the outbreak of Civil War, enlisted into Confederate service as part of Louisiana governor Thomas O. Moore's staff; captain, 1st Louisiana Artillery, March 1861; colonel, 13th Louisiana Infantry, September 1861; at Shiloh led several attempts to break the infamous Hornets' Nest but was repulsed each time; upon the injury of Brig. Gen. Daniel W. Adams, assumed command of the Louisiana Brigade; later fought at Perryville, Murfreesboro, Chickamauga, and Chattanooga; brigadier general, January 1864, for service at Chickamauga; served under Gen. John Bell Hood during the Atlanta campaign and in Hood's invasion of Tennessee; in February 1865 went with his brigade to Mobile and garrisoned Spanish Fort; defended that post for some time in early April before overwhelming Federal numbers forced an evacuation; later surrendered with Lt. Gen. Richard Taylor's army at Cuba Station in May 1865; opened a law practice in New Orleans after the war and was elected to Congress in 1872, though denied his seat due to Reconstruction policies; elected again in 1875 and served in the House of Representatives until 1882; elected to the U.S. Senate, serving from 1883 to 1892; during this time helped establish Tulane University and served as president of the Board of Administrators; he died in the winter of 1892 at Hot Springs, Arkansas. Randall Lee Gibson was a well-traveled, intelligent man with capable soldierly skills who spent the later years of his life as one of Louisiana's dedicated civil servants.

do-laced upper reaches of Mobile Bay. The defending Rebel force at first numbered one man for every yard of front. But Maury reduced that ratio on the fourth day of the siege when he transferred the brigade of Alabama boy-reserves to Blakely and replaced it with a few veterans. Left to do the digging, move ammunition, place the heavy guns, repair damage, and extend the main lines—as well as simply fight—were but fifteen hundred soldiers and less than three hundred cannoneers. This comparative handful fought all day and then dug all night, dropping their muskets only to pick up their spades.

For the Union soldiers outside the fort, life was not much different than it was for the Rebels inside—both were closely linked to the shovel. They were entrenched in ravines and under crests of hills, and for them, like the Confederates, their duty called for hours of sleepless vigilance, a routine of incessant toil night and day, digging tunnels and trenches, constructing batteries, building earthworks and fortifications, and inching the guns ever closer. It was a stalking operation with all of the labor incident to a siege. "The pick and the spade always accompanied the picket," one Federal officer said. The Sixteenth Corps's medical director, W.H. Thome, called it "fatigue duty in the trenches."

The front lines of the opposing armies, within shouting distance of one another, quickly settled into a routine. The soldiers were soon on such intimate terms that when the Rebels were about to fire their mortars they cried out: "Look out, Yank, we're going to fire." An explosion would be followed by the rushing noise of an answering mortar shell and with it a shout of warning from the Union lines: "Look out, Johnny Reb, she's coming."

The sharpshooters on both sides, however, were less considerate, picking their enemies off—particularly the officers— like wild game.

By April 4, thirty-eight Union siege guns and thirty-seven mortars were trained on Spanish Fort. To answer this weight of metal and firepower, the Confederates had about forty guns, the heavy ones named in honor of their officers' ladies, the names written in large letters placarded on each gun—"The Lady Gibson," "The Lady Slocum," "The Lady Maury." The gunners spoke of them with affection, by their names, and were always exceedingly polite and complimentary to them.

The Confederates also named the Federal guns, with which they were becoming daily more familiar. One they named "Anna Maria," another "Sarah Jane," and another "Elizabeth Ann." When one fired, the picket would shout, "Look out, boys, Anna Maria is going to speak." The word would pass down the line and all knew in advance the direction the shot was coming from and ducked for appropriate cover. When one of their own ladies was about to "speak," they said: "Ah, my lads! Look out for the Lady Slocum; when she speaks the Yanks must hush up and hide." The damage done, in any case, was generally less than ladylike.

In this way the besieged garrison of Spanish Fort struck back, exposing their stalking enemy to unrelenting daytime fire of artillery and musketry, much of it well directed. "Not an hour, scarcely a moment in the day but the missiles from their guns were flying thick and fast," a Union colonel recalled. The Rebel sharpshooters were untiring. It was impossible to move without risking danger.

Gibson kept up a bombardment of a different sort on Maury in Mobile, burying the general in an avalanche of requests for things that might help him hold out. He pled for more picks and shovels, more Negro slaves to wield them, a launch, a gunboat, half a dozen grindstones, more guns, more mortars, a company of sappers and miners, an ironclad, "subterra shells" (underground mines), hand grenades, more troops, and finally for Maury himself. And Maury sent all he could.

Daily, Canby tightened the screws. By April 8, nearly all of Gibson's artillery had been silenced. Federal guns had multiplied to nearly one hundred and had become ever more deadly. The pressure on the Confederate flanks, particularly the left, had become all but unbearable.

April 8 dawned, and all the Federal "ladies" simultaneously began speaking—shrieking, as a Union naval officer described such discord, "like a thousand devils." "Hellfire," a Rebel cannoneer remembered,

> rained upon us from front and flank and rear and top, from field guns, siege guns, ship guns and mortars; such a tempest of shot and shell as defies description. Think of seventy-five or a hundred guns massed in a semi-circle thick around us; think of those huge mortars belching forth their monstrous contents

down upon us; think of the fleet in our rear pouring
its fire into our back. . . . The very air was hot. The
din was so great it distracted our senses. We could
hardly hear each other speak and could hardly tell
what we were doing. The cracking of musketry, the
unbroken roaring of artillery, the yelling and shrieking of the shells, the bellowing boom of the mortars,
the dense shroud of sulphurous smoke thickening
around us—it was thought the mouth of the pit had
yawned and the uproar of the damned was about us.

It was useless to try to answer such infernal shrieking.
There was no safety any longer in the bombproofs or shelters.
The Rebels could see every Union cannonball as it left the
mortar's mouth, so they simply deserted their works and went
out into the exposed space behind their own silenced guns to
devote their day to a grim game of deadly dodge ball.

One man was particularly skilled at watching the bombs
leave the mortars, mentally calculating their arcs, and predict-
ing with supernatural accuracy where they would land. All the
other cannoneers, not blessed with this useful insight themselves, clustered about him and at his signal ran where he ran.
"Sing out, S——," shouted the officers, who were brave but
also wise, "and tell us which way to run." And when he sang
out, they all ran with him, without question.

By late in the afternoon of April 8, the game was up. The
breakthrough on the Confederate left came at about five
o'clock. As night closed in, there was nothing left for the
Rebels but to get out or be taken prisoner. But getting out
looked impossible to many of these weary defenders.

What they did not know was that it had never been Maury's
intention to sacrifice the garrison. His orders to Gibson had
been to abandon Spanish Fort the moment it was in danger of
capture. It was now night—a hazy moonlit night, damp and
still—and the danger was palpable.

Gibson had thought often of what a difficult task it was to decide when the time to withdraw had come. But it had clearly come now, and he recognized it. He ordered the guns spiked and issued the last of his remaining stores to the men. The sick and wounded were carried to the edge of the fort. The garrison was mustered, and at nine o'clock Gibson sent a final wire to Maury: "I am beginning to retire by the treadway."

The young general had built a narrow treadway, nearly a mile long, across the marsh behind Spanish Fort for their escape. Though heavy Federal batteries now commanded its entire length, the path was concealed by high grass and covered with moss. Moreover, Canby was not expecting an escape attempt.

The Confederates began pulling off their shoes and noiselessly exiting along the treadway. It was a movement that could not be hurried. The long line slipped quietly out under the barrels of the Union cannon, so close to the enemy pickets that they could hear them talking. At the end of the long treadway, Gibson's men found Maury's launches waiting to take them to Fort Blakely and then on to Mobile.

The next morning, Canby found only six hundred prisoners who had not made it out of Spanish Fort. The main part of the garrison had escaped.

Frederick Steele and his troops, slogging through the mud and over the corduroy roads from Pensacola, had arrived in front of Fort Blakely on April 5 and put it under siege. For four days, the Federals had endured a stubborn Confederate resistance from the prickly tempered Liddell. But on April 9, reinforced by the soldiers of A. J. Smith's "wandering tribe," which had hurried to his lines after Spanish Fort fell the night before, Steele attacked.

The Confederate position in crescent-shaped Fort Blakely stretched for two and a half miles and bristled with nine strong redoubts connected by rifle pits filled with sharpshooters and skirmishers. Its front was guarded by palisades and barricades of heavy timber and abatis (forward pointing branches sharpened into spikes). In some places entangling webs of telegraph wire were strung along the approach, and torpedoes and subterra shells were buried in the ground. An assault was not a pleasant prospect.

But Steele launched one about 5:30 in the afternoon under a heavy cover of artillery fire and musketry. The sun was just dropping into the bay to the Confederate rear. Despite the exploding torpedoes, the barricades, and the abatis, the power of the attack was irresistible. The fort was carried in about twenty minutes.

As Federal troops stormed over the breastworks, Confederate sergeant John J. Gray aimed his 12-pounder James rifle, charged with canister, directly down the line and let fly through the packed Union ranks. This Parthian shot was the last one fired by the Confederates at Mobile and one of the last of the war, for Robert E. Lee even then was surrendering to Ulysses S. Grant at Appomattox.

There was no treadway to freedom at Blakely as there had been at Spanish Fort, and Liddell and more than three thousand of his defenders were captured in the sudden Federal charge. Two smaller works nearby were immediately evacuated and blown up. The rivers were swept for torpedoes and the fleet, at last, occupied the upper bay in front of the city of Mobile itself.

One Confederate wrote that it had been a lovely spring day, but the night was "a sorry one for all of us."

8
SUNSET ON THE GULF

Maury had done all he could. He had held out for three weeks. But now his effective force was reduced to less than five thousand men. His ammunition was nearly exhausted by the two sieges, and there was no longer a Confederacy to send him more. Mobile and its thirty thousand citizens were at the mercy of Union firepower from the land and from the water. An obstinate, protracted, last-ditch defense now seemed senseless.

Mary Waring, only twenty years old, awoke in Mobile on the morning of April 12 "with a most deserted and desolate" feeling. That morning before daylight, Maury had begun marching his army out of the city. As he left with the rear guard, he sent word under a white flag to the Union fleet that the Union army might now enter and take bloodless possession of Mobile.

Mobile's mayor, R. H. Slough, accompanied by members of the city council in carriages with a large white flag flying,

Union Troops Entering Mobile

drove out to a point near the old Magnolia Race Course on the Bay Shield Road, met the Federal army, and surrendered his city. At 12:30 P.M. the U.S. flag was hoisted over the customhouse. That afternoon Gordon Granger marched up Conception Street to the strains of "Yankee Doodle" as Mary Waring and Mobile sadly watched.

To Mary's prejudiced young eyes, the Yankee invaders differed "in the greatest degree from our own poor dear soldiers—the commonest, dirtiest-looking set I ever saw." She had lived in Mobile all of her life, and at that moment she felt like a stranger in her own city. But even so, she admitted that the invaders were quiet, courteous, orderly, and apparently intended them no harm.

The day Granger entered Mobile, General Canby ordered six thousand cavalry from Pensacola to intercept Maury. But they could not cross the rain-swollen Alabama and Tombigbee Rivers, and the little Rebel army slipped untouched into Meridian, Mississippi.

Mobile was lost, but there was still fight in Canby's diminutive Confederate friend. Maury was preparing to march overland to join another old friend, Confederate general Joseph E. Johnston, who was opposing William T. Sherman's Union army marching through the Carolinas. But news of Lee's surrender at Appomattox reached Maury in Cuba, Mississippi, followed

RICHARD TAYLOR

Richard Taylor: born Kentucky 1826; son of president and Mexican War hero Zachary Taylor and brother in law of Confederate president Jefferson Davis; studied at Yale; became a successful sugar planter in Louisiana; elected colonel, 9th Louisiana Infantry, at the outbreak of the Civil War and went with the regiment to Virginia, arriving too late for Manassas; promoted to brigadier general, 1861; commanded the Louisiana Brigade in Maj. Gen. Thomas J. "Stonewall" Jackson's Shenandoah Valley campaign of 1862; present but not active during the Seven Days' Battles before Richmond; promoted to major general and assigned to command the District of Western Louisiana in 1862; unsuccessfully opposed Maj. Gen. Nathaniel P. Banks's Bayou Teche expedition in 1863 but turned back Banks' Red River campaign the following spring; after a heated exchange in which he criticized his commander, Lt. Gen. E. Kirby Smith, for not following up on his success, asked to be relieved; promoted to lieutenant general and assigned to command the Department of Alabama, Mississippi, and East Louisiana; following the disaster at Nashville, temporarily succeeded Gen. John B. Hood in command of the Army of Tennessee, most of which he forwarded to the Carolinas to opposed Maj. Gen. William T. Sherman's advance; after the fall of Mobile, surrendered the last remaining Confederate force east of the Mississippi to Maj. Gen. E.R.S. Canby on May 4, 1865; after the war was active in Democratic politics and vigorously opposed Reconstruction policies. He died at New York in 1879 after completing his *Destruction and Reconstruction,* one of the finest participant memoirs to be produced. Without any formal military training, General Taylor proved to be a most able commander. The Confederate repulse of the Red River campaign, though largely overlooked, was a major achievement.

by word that Confederate president Jefferson Davis had been captured. With these reports, Maury simply halted his little force and awaited the final issue of events.

When news of Lee's surrender reached the Gulf region, Canby and Lt. Gen. Richard Taylor agreed to meet at a place ten miles north of Mobile near the railway. Taylor appropriated a railroad handcar and with a single staff officer pumped up the line, finding Canby and a large escort of staff and other officers waiting for him. Among them, Taylor saw and greeted for the first time in four years many old friends, Canby included.

The Union contingent had thoughtfully brought the drinks and food—pastries, champagne frappe, and other "delights." As they took their seats, a military band struck up "Hail Columbia," the Union anthem, which Canby gallantly interrupted with a request for "Dixie," the Confederate anthem. As its last strains died away, Taylor asked for "Hail Columbia" once more. The bonds that had been severed for four years were beginning to reknit.

But this was only a preliminary meeting to agree to a truce. It was not until news of Johnston's surrender to Sherman in North Carolina arrived a month later that Taylor finally called it quits. He then ordered Maury and the other scattered remnants of his command to return to Meridian. It was time for them to surrender too.

The night before he marched his ragged troops into Meridian, Maury addressed them one final time. "Soldiers: Our last march is almost ended. To-morrow we shall lay down the arms we have borne for four years to defend our rights—to win our liberties. . . . Conscious that we have played our part like men, confident of the righteousness of our cause, without regret for our past action, and without despair of the future let us to-morrow, with the dignity of the veterans who are the last to surrender, perform the duty which has been assigned to us."

The following day, Maury surrendered all he had to Canby for the second time in their careers. He doubtless hoped it would be the last. On the night of May 13, after the surrender was completed, the musicians of General Gibson's Louisiana brigade, probably the only Confederate band left in the world, played Maury a last sad farewell serenade.

It was finally over. "Puss in Boots" had closed out the war along the Gulf of Mexico.

APPENDIX A

ORGANIZATION OF CONFEDERATE TROOPS
Confederate Forces at Mobile, Alabama

Mobile
Maj. Gen. Dabney H. Maury, Commander

Fort Morgan
Brig. Gen. Richard L. Page, Commander
1st Alabama Battalion of Artillery
21st Alabama, (1 company)
1st Tennessee

Fort Gaines
Col. Charles D. Anderson, Commander
21st Alabama, (6 companies)
1st Alabama Battalion of Artillery, (2 companies)
Pelham Cadets
Reserves and Marines

Fort Powell
Lt. Col. James M. Williams, Commander
21st Alabama, (2 companies)
Culpeper's South Carolina Battery, (part)

APPENDIX B

ORGANIZATION OF UNION FORCES
Union Forces at Mobile, Alabama

Union Forces

Military Division of West Mississippi
Maj. Gen. Edward R. S. Canby, Commander

District of South Alabama
Maj. Gen. Gordon Granger, Commander

Mobile Bay Forces
Brig. Gen. George H. Gordon, Commander

Brigade Commanders
Col. Joseph Bailey
Col. Joshua J. Guppey
Col. George w. Clark
Col. Henry Bertram
Col. George D. Robinson

Infantry
77th Illinois
94th Illinois
67th Indiana
20th Iowa
34th Iowa
38th Iowa
161st New York
96th Ohio
20th Wisconsin
96th U.S.C.T.
97th U.S.C.T

Cavalry
3rd Maryland
Company A, 2nd Maine
Company M, 14th New York

Artillery
1st Indiana Heavy, (battalion)
6th Michigan Heavy
Battery A, 2nd Illinois
2nd Connecticut Battery
17th Ohio Battery

APPENDIX C

CONFEDERATE AND UNITED STATES SHIPS

All ship information taken from
Sliverstone, Paul H. *Warships of the Civil War Navies.*
Annapolis: United States Naval Institute Press, 1989.

Confederate Warships Mentioned

Admiral Franklin Buchanan, Commanding

CSS *Gaines*
Gunboat
(Built in 1862)

Dimensions: 863 tons, 202' length, 38' beam.
    Speed: 10 knots
    Armament: 1 7" R, 1 6" R, 2 32-pdr R, 2 32-pdr SB

War Record: Engaged at the Battle of Mobile Bay on August 5, 1864 and
    ran aground to prevent capture after the battle.

CSS *Morgan*
Gunboat
(Built in 1862)

Dimensions: 863 tons, 202' length, 38' beam.
    Speed: 10 knots
    Armament: 1 7" R, 1 6" R, 2 32-pdr R, 2 32-pdr SB

War Record: Engaged at the Battle of Mobile Bay August 5, 1864, served
    in an engagement near Blakely, were it received damage, in
    early 1865. May of the same year the *Morgan* surrendered
    to Federal forces.

CSS *Selma*
Gunboat, converted coastal packet steamer
(Built 1856, acquired April 22, 1861)

Dimensions: 320 tons B, 252' length, 30' beam.
    Speed: 9 knots
    Crew: 99
Armament: 2 9" R, 1 8" R, 1 6" R

War Record: The *Selma* saw action twice in late 1861 as it engaged the
USS *Massachussets* and USS *Montgomery* off Mobile.
Engaged at the Battle of Mobile Bay on August 5, 1864
were she hit a snag and sank. She refloated and would surrender on that same day to Union forces. The *Selma*
received its commission to the United States Navy after its
surrender.

CSS *Tennessee*
Modified Columbia type Ironclad.
(Launched October 1862, commissioned February 16, 1864)

Dimensions: 1,273 tons, 209' length, 48' beam.
    Speed: 6 knots
    Crew: 133
Armament: 2 7" R, 4 6.4" R

War Record: Built in Selma, Alabama, the *Tennessee* saw action at the
Battle of Mobile on August 5, 1864 as the flagship of Admiral
Buchanan's Mobile fleet. As the battle wore on she was disabled and forced to surrender to the United States Navy.
Once in the hands of Federal forces the *Tennessee* was commissioned on August 19, 1864 in the United States Navy on
participated in the attack on Fort Morgan four days later.

United States Warships Mentioned

Rear Admiral David G. Farragut, Commanding
Fleet Captain, Captain Percival Drayton

USS *Brooklyn*
Screw Sloop, ship rigged.
(Launched July 27, 1858, Commissioned January 26, 1859)

Dimensions: 2,532 tons D, 2,070 tons B, 233' length, 43' beam, 16'3" draft.
Speed: 11.5 knots
Crew: 335
Armament: 1864: 1 100-pdr R, 22 9" SB, 1 30-pdr R.

War Record: The *Brooklyn* saw tons of action during the Civil War, working as part of the West Gulf Blockading Squadron from
1861 until 1864. During this period, she engaged with CSN
ships following the pass of the New Orleans forts in April of
1862, the following month she aided in the attack on the
Grand Gulf in Mississippi. In addition, during 1862, the
Brooklyn took an active role in the passing of the batteries
at Vicksburg and the attack on Vicksburg. On January 10
and February 24 of 1863 the ship helped conduct a bombardment on Galveston. A year later, on August 5, 1864
the *Brooklyn* engaged at the Battle of Mobile Bay and in the
bombardment of Ft. Morgan during the entire month. From
October of 1864 until January of 1865 she served in the
North Atlantic Blockading Squadron and took part in both
attacks on Ft. Fisher, North Carolina. Overall the *Brooklyn*
would take nine prizes during the war.

USS *Chickasaw*
Double-turret monitor, Milwaukee Class
(Launched February 10, 1864, Commissioned May 14, 1864)

Dimensions: 1,300 tons D, 970 tons B, 229' length, 56' beam.
Speed: 9 knots
Crew: 138
Armament: 8" turrets, 1 .5" deck

War Record: The *Chickasaw* served as part of the West Gulf Blockading
Squadron, fought in the Battle of Mobile Bay on August 5,
1864, and took part in the bombardment of Ft. Morgan
during the same month. The ship was decommissioned on
July 6, 1865.

USS *Galena*

Third of three experimental Ironclads
(Launched February 14, 1862, Commissioned April 21, 1862)

Dimensions: 950 tons D, 738 tons B, 210' length, 36' beam.
    Speed: 8 knots
    Crew: 150
Armament: April 1864: 1 100-pdr R, 1 30-pdr R, 8 9" SB, 1 12-pdr H.

War Record: Began her war service as part of the North Atlantic
    Blockading Squadron, the *Galena* took part in the engage-
    ment at Drewry's Bluff, Virginia were it received sever dam-
    age. The ship remained out of commission until February
    15, 1864 when it was re-commissioned and seat afloat as
    part of the West Gulf Blockading Squadron. *Galena* saw
    action on August 5, 1864 at the Battle of Mobile Bay and
    engaged in the bombardment of Ft. Morgan all during that
    same month, during which time she was part of the East
    Gulf Blockading Squadron. In April of the following year the
    Galena joined the North Atlantic Blockading Squadron, but
    only two months later she was decommissioned.

USS *Hartford*

Screw Sloop, ship rigged.
(Launched November 22, 1858, commissioned May 27, 1859)

Dimensions: 2,900 tons D; 1,900 tons B, 225' length, 44' beam, 17'2" draft.
    Speed: 13.5 knots
    Crew: 310
Armament: 2 100-pdr R, 18 9" SB, 1 30-pdr R, 3 13-pdr H.

War Record: The *Hartford* spent the most of the war as the flagship for
    the West Gulf Blockading Squadron and saw action in many
    different places. In 1862 she passed New Orleans forts and
    engaged C.S.N. ships in April. That same the *Hartford*
    passed the batteries at Vicksburg and fought with the CSS
    Arkansas on July 15, 1862. She also took part in the pas-
    sage of Port Hudson, Louisiana, Grand Gulf, Mississippi
    and the bombardment of Ft Powell, Mobile Bay. On August
    5, 1864 the ship engaged in the Battle of Mobile Bay and
    followed it with participation in the bombardment of Ft.
    Morgan during the same month. The *Hartford* took one
    prize during the war.

USS *Itasca*

Unadilla Class, Screw Gunboat
(Launched October 1, 1861, Commissioned November 28, 1861)

Dimensions: 691 tons D; 507 tons B, 158'4" length, 28' beam, 9'6" draft.
Speed: 10 knots
Crew: 114
Armament: 1 11" SB, 2 32-pdr/27, 1 20-pdr R.

War Record: The *Itasca* served in the both the Gulf Blockading Squadron and the West Gulf Blockading Squadron during 1862. She took part in the chain across the Mississippi River and also made her way past the forts at New Orleans. The ship would find problems during the bombardment of Grand Gulf, Mississippi as she was damaged in a few areas. Late 1862 the *Itasca* took part in operations around Donaldsonville, Louisiana and a year later she served in the blockade of Galveston. On August 5, 1864 she engaged at the Battle of Mobile Bay and took part in the days to follow in the bombardment of Ft. Morgan. The *Itasca* took five prizes during the war.

USS *Kennebec*

Unadilla Class, Screw Gunboat
(Launched October 5, 1861, Commissioned February 8, 1862)

Dimensions: 691 tons D; 507 tons B, 158'4" length, 28' beam, 9'6" draft.
Speed: 10 knots
Crew: 114
Armament: 1 11" SB, 1 30-pdr R, 1 24-pdr H, 1 12-pdr.

War Record: Served in the West Gulf Blockading Squadron in 1862, the *Kennebec* saw action as it passed the New Orleans forts and fought with Confederate ships. Also, she engaged in the passage past batteries at Vicksburg and pulled blockade duties during late 1862 and throughout 1863. She participated in the Battle of Mobile Bay on August 5, 1864, afterward the *Kennebec* took part in blockade duty off of Galveston, Texas. She claimed five prizes during the war.

USS *Lackawanna*
Lackawanna Class, Screw Sloop
(Launched August 9, 1862, Commissioned January 8, 1863)

Dimensions: 2,526 tons D; 1,533 tons B, 237' length, 38'2" beam,
16'6" draft.
Speed: 11 knots
Crew: 205
Armament: 1 150-pdr R, 2 11" SB, 4 9" SB, 1 50-pdr R, 2 24-pdr R, 2
12-pdr H, 2 12-pdr R.

War Record: She served in the West Gulf Blockading Squadron in 1863
and engaged at the Battle of Mobile Bay in August. During
that month, she also participated in the bombardment of Ft.
Morgan. The *Lackawanna* took two prizes during the war.

USS *Manhattan*
Canonicus Class, Monitors
(Launched October 14, 1863, Commissioned June 6, 1864)

Dimensions: 2,100 tons D; 1,034 tons B, 223' length, 43'4" beam,
13'6" draft.
Speed: 8 knots
Crew: 85
Armament: 2 15" SB guns

War Record: The *Manhattan* worked in the Gulf Blockading Squadron in
1863 and fought at the Battle of Mobile Bay the following
year. She took part in the bombardment of Ft. Morgan during the month of August of the same year. A year later she
was laid up ending her Civil War career.

USS *Metacomet*
Sassacus Class, wooden hull, Side-Wheel Gunboat
(Launched March 7, 1863, Commissioned January 4, 1864)

Dimensions: 1,173 tons D; 974 tons B, 240' length, 35' beam.
  Speed: 13 knots
  Crew: 200
  Armament: 2 100-pdr R, 4 9" SB, 2 12-pdr R, 2 24-pdr.

War Record: She spent 1864 in the West Gulf Blockading Squadron and
engaged at the Battle of Mobile Bay on August 5, 1864
were she received damage from the CSS *Selma*. A few days
later the *Metacomet* would engage in the bombardment of
Ft. Morgan, Mobile Bay. The United State Navy decommissioned the ship on August 18, 1865. During the war the
Metacomet laid claim to five prizes.

USS *Monongahela*
Barkentine rigged, Screw Sloop
(Launched July 10, 1862, Commissioned January 15, 1863)

Dimensions: 2,078 tons D; 1,378 tons B, 225' length, 38' beam, 15'1"
    draft.
  Speed: 12 knots
  Crew: 176
  Armament: 1 150-pdr R, 5 32-pdr/57, 2 11" SB, 2 24-pdr R, 4 12-pdr R.

War Record: In 1863 the *Monongahela* served in the West Gulf
Blockading Squadron and participated in lots of engage-
ments. She engaged in an attempt to pass Port Hudson,
Louisiana in March of 1863, but was unsuccessful and end-
ed up receiving damage after being run aground. In July,
she took part in the bombardment below Donaldsonville,
Louisiana and the bombardment of Whitehall Pt.,
Louisiana. In late 1863, the *Monongahela* set out on the
expedition to Brazos Santiago, Rio Grande, Texas. On
August 5, 1864 she engaged the CSS *Tennessee* at the
Battle of Mobile Bay, and four days later began to bombard
Ft. Morgan, Mobile Bay. She claimed all her four of her
prizes on November 5, 1863.

USS *Octorara*
Side-Wheel Gunboat, Double-Ender
(Launched December 7, 1861, Commissioned February 28, 1862)

Dimensions: 981 tons D; 829 tons B, 193'2" length, 34'6" beam,
4'10" draft.
Speed: 11 knots
Crew: 118
Armament: 1 100-pdr R, 3 9" SB, 2 32-pdr/33, 4 24-pdr H.

War Record: In 1862 the *Octorara* served in both the North Atlantic
Blockading Squadron and the West Gulf Blockading
Squadron, while taking part in the passage past the batteries at Vicksburg were the helm jammed in June. Early 1864
she participated in the bombardment of Ft. Powell, Mobile
Bay. In August she engaged during the Battle of Mobile Bay
were she was damaged, but not enough to keep her out of
the bombardment a few days later on Ft. Morgan. January
of 1865, the *Octorara* attacked the CSS *St. Patrick* and a
few months later took part in the capture of Mobile. During
the war she claimed 12 prizes, and received her decommis-
sion on August 5, 1865.

USS *Oneida*
Iroquois Class, Schooner rigged, Screw Sloop
(Launched November 20, 1861, Commissioned February 28, 1862)

Dimensions: 1,488 tons D: 1,1032 tons B, 198'10" length, 33'10" beam,
13' draft.
Speed: 11.5 knots
Crew: 123
Armament: 2 11" SB, 6 8"/63, 1 30-pdr R, 2 24-pdr H, 1 12-pdr H.

War Record: Part of the West Gulf Blockading Squadron, involved in the
passage of New Orleans forts, occupied the Natchez, participated in bombardment of Grand Gulf, Mississippi, made
passage through the batteries at Vicksburg, and engaged
the CSS *Arkansas* all in 1862. The *Oneida* took part in the
blockade of Mobile and engaged during the Battle of Mobile
Bay on August 5, 1864.

USS *Ossipee*
Ossipee Class, Screw Sloop
(Launched November 16, 1861, Commissioned November 6, 1862)

Dimensions: 1,934 tons D; 1,240 tons B, 205' length, 38' beam, 16'7" draft.
    Speed: 12 knots
    Crew: 160
    Armament: 1 100-pdr R, 1 11" SB, 3 30-pdr R, 6 32-pdr/57, 1 12-pdr SB, 1 12-pdr R.

War Record: The *Ossipee* worked in the North Atlantic Blockading Squadron from 1862 until 1863, then joined the West Gulf Blockading Squadron in May of 1863 and was engaged at the Battle of Mobile in August of 1864. She also took part in the bombardment of Ft. Morgan, Mobile Bay. Throughout the war the *Ossipee* claimed three prizes.

USS *Port Royal*
Side-Wheel Gunboat, Double-Ender
(Launched January 17, 1862, Commissioned April 26, 1862)

Dimensions: 1,163 tons D; 805 tons B, 209' length, 35' beam, 7'8" draft.
    Speed: 9.5 knots
    Crew: 131
    Armament: 1 100-pdr R, 1 10" SB, 2 9" SB, 2 50-pdr R, 2 24-pdr H, 1 12-pdr SB.

War Record: The *Port Royal* served in the North Atlantic Blockading Squadron during 1862 and 1863. She saw action at Sewells Point, Virginia and at Drewry's Bluff, Virginia in 1862 and a year later participated in the bombardment of Ft. Wagner. From 1864 to 1865 the *Port Royal* belonged to the East Gulf Blockading Squadron and took part in the bombardment of Ft. Powell in early 1864. Engaged at the Battle of Mobile Bay in August of the same year and took her shots at Ft. Morgan after the battle. The vessel was decommissioned in May of 1866, after the war in which she took two prizes.

USS *Richmond*
Screw Sloop, ship rigged
(Launched January 26, 1860, Commissioned October 1860)

Dimensions: 2,700 tons D; 1,929 tons B, 225' length, 42'6" beam, 17'5"
draft.
Speed: 9.5 knots
Crew: 260
Armament: 1 100-pdr R, 1 30-pdr R, 18 9" SB.

War Record: Prior to the war the *Richmond* served time in the
Mediterranean and spent time in 1861 searching the
Caribbean for the CSS *Sumter*. She would take many hits
during her service in the war, a service that began with an
engagement with the CSS *Manassas* in late 1861, followed
by participation in the bombardment of Pensacola, Florida,
a passage of the forts of New Orleans and then involvement
in the passage of the batteries at Vicksburg. All of this
occurred before July of 1862 when the vessel took even
more blows while engaging the CSS *Arkansas* above
Vicksburg. The *Richmond* also had an active role in the
occupation of Baton Rouge and the attempted pass of Port
Hudson in March of 1863. On August 5, 1864 she engaged
at the Battle of Mobile Bay and a few days later she participated in the bombardment of Ft. Morgan. Her last engagement would be in April of 1865 when she clashed with the
CSS *Webb* off of the coast near New Orleans.

USS *Seminole*
Narragansett Class, Screw Sloop
(Launched June 25, 1859, Commissioned April 25 1860)

Dimensions: 1,235 tons D; 804 tons B, 208' length, 32'2" beam,
11'6" draft.
Speed: 11 knots
Crew: 120
Armament: 1 11" SB, 1 30-pdr R, 6 32-pdr/43, 1 12-pdr R.

War Record: Served at the Brazil Station before the start of the war, in
1861 she moved into the Atlantic Blockading Squadron and
served some time in the Potomac Flotilla. The *Seminole*
participated in the bombardment at Freestone Point,
Virginia in September of 1861 and a month later relocated
to the South Atlantic Blockading Squadron and took part in

the occupation of Port Royal, South Carolina. 1862 proved to be a busy year for the *Seminole*, she was involved with the capture of Fernandina, Florida, Brunswick, St. Simmons, and Jekyl islands, Georgia, and engaged at Sewells Point, Virginia. In July of 1863 she joined the West Gulf Blockading Squadron, and a year later participated in the Battle of Mobile Bay as well as the bombardment of Ft. Morgan. The vessel was decommissioned in August of 1865. During the war she claimed six prizes.

USS *Tecumseh*
Canonicus Class, Monitor
(Launched September 12, 1863, Commissioned April 19, 1864)

Dimensions: 2,100 tons D; 1,034 tons B, 233' length, 43'4" beam, 13'6" draft.
Speed: 8 knots
Crew: 85
Armament: 2 15" SB guns.

War Record: The *Tecumseh* served in the North Atlantic Blockading Squadron in 1864 and also took part in the James River flotilla. She engaged at Howletts, Trents Reach, Virginia before being moved into the West Gulf Blockading Squadron were she would engage at the Battle of Mobile Bay on August 5, 1864 and hit a torpedo (mine) and sank.

USS *Winnebago*
Milwaukee Class, Double-turret Monitor
(Launched July 4, 1863, Commissioned April 27, 1864)

Dimensions: 1,300 tons D, 970 tons B, 229' length, 56' beam, 6' draft.
Speed: 9 knots
Crew: 138
Armament: 4 11" SB

War Record: Began service in the Mississippi Squadron and moved into the West Gulf Blockading Squadron by July of 1864. Engaged at the Battle of Mobile Bay on August 5, 1864 and received lots of damage. Four days later she participated in the bombardment of Ft. Morgan. The vessel was decommissioned in September of 1869.

ABOUT THE BIOGRAPHICAL SKETCHES

The biographical sketches that accompany the photographs in this volume were derived from numerous sources and were written by Paul Cochran, David Coffey, Daniel Price, Brooks Sommer, and Grady McWhiney.

FURTHER READING

There are two reasonably recent, detailed, book-length monographs of the battles of Mobile and Mobile Bay—Arthur W. Bergeron's *Confederate Mobile* (Jackson: University Press of Mississippi, 1991) and Chester G. Hearn's *Mobile Bay and the Mobile Campaign: The Last Great Battles of the Civil War* (Jefferson, N.C.: McFarland, 1993). Both are excellent.

Numerous biographies of David Glasgow Farragut exist. Charles Lee Lewis's two-volume work, *David Glasgow Farragut: Our First Admiral* (Annapolis: U.S. Naval Institute, 1943), is the most authoritative and detailed. But *The Life of David Glasgow Farragut, First Admiral of the United States Navy, Embodying His Journal and Letters*, written and com-piled by his son, Loyall Farragut (New York: D. Appleton, 1879), is well worth reading. Other works on the admiral, all worthy of notice, are listed in the section of sources consulted below.

Charles Lee Lewis has also written the standard biography of Franklin Buchanan, *Admiral Franklin Buchanan: Fearless Man of Action* (Baltimore: Norman, Remington, 1929). An excellent new biography is also now available, Craig L. Symonds's *Confederate Admiral: The Life and Wars of Franklin Buchanan* (Annapolis: Naval Institute Press, 1999).

Dabney Herndon Maury and E.R.S. Canby have been gener-ally neglected by biographers, but Maury's memoir, *Recollections of a Virginian in the Mexican, Indian, and Civil Wars* (New York: Charles Scribner's Sons, 1894), is delightful.

OTHER SOURCES CONSULTED

Andrews, C.C. *History of the Campaign of Mobile.* New York: D. Van Nostrand, 1867.

Barnes, James. *David G. Farragut.* Boston: Small, Maynard, 1899.

Brother, Charles. "The Journal of Pvt. Charles Brother, USMC, on the USS *Hartford.*" In *Two Naval Journals: 1864,* edited by C. Carter Smith Jr. Chicago: Wyvern Press of S.F.E., 1964.

Cameron, William Lochiel. "The Battles Opposite Mobile." *Confederate Veteran* 23 (July 1915): 305–8.

Clark, Charles E. *My Fifty Years in the Navy.* Boston: Little, Brown, 1917.

Conrad, Daniel B. "Capture of the C.S. Ram *Tennessee* in Mobile Bay, August, 1864." *Southern Historical Society Papers* 19 (1891): 62–82. This is a rich source for what was going on aboard the Confederate ram during the battle in the bay.

Cox, Benjamin B. "Mobile in the War between the States." *Confederate Veteran* 24 (May 1916): 209–13.

Cullum, George W. Cullum File, Class of 1846. U.S. Military Academy Library, West Point, N.Y.

Dictionary of American Biography. Edited by Allen Johnson and Dumas Malone. 20 vols. New York: Charles Scribner's Sons, 1964.

Harrington, Purnell Frederick. "The Storming of Mobile Bay." Edited by Richard R. Duncan. *Alabama Historical Quarterly* 40 (spring/summer 1978): 6–19.

Harrison, Mary Douglass [Waring]. *Miss Waring's Journal: 1863 and 1865, being the Diary of Miss Mary Waring of Mobile, during the Final Days of the War between the States.* Edited by Thad Holt Jr. Chicago: Wyvern Press of S.F.E., 1964.

Headley, Joel Tyler. *Farragut and Our Naval Commanders.* New York: E.B. Treat, 1866.

Hults, Ellsworth H. "Aboard the *Galena* at Mobile." *Civil War Times Illustrated* 10 (April 1971): 12–21; (May 1971): 28–40.

Hutchinson, William F. "The Bay Fight: A Sketch of the Battle of Mobile Bay, August 5th, 1864." In *Personal Narratives of Events in the War of the Rebellion.* Vol. 1, no. 8. Rhode Island Soldiers and Sailors Historical Society, 1878–79. Reprint, Wilmington, N.C.: Broadfoot, 1993.

Irwin, Richard B. "Land Operations against Mobile." In *Battles and Leaders of the Civil War,* edited by Robert Underwood Johnson and Clarence Clough Buel. Vol. 4. 1887. Reprint, Secaucus, N.J.: Castle, n.d.

Johnston, James D. "The Battle of Mobile Bay." *Southern Historical Society Papers* 9 (1881): 471–76.

_____. "The Ram 'Tennessee' at Mobile Bay." In *Battles and Leaders of the Civil War,* edited by Robert Underwood Johnson and Clarence Clough Buel. Vol. 4. 1887. Reprint, Secaucus, N.J.: Castle, n.d. These two accounts are by the captain of the *Tennessee.*

Jones, Virgil Carrington. *The Civil War at Sea.* Vol. 3, *The Final Effort.* 1962. Reprint, Wilmington, N.C.: Broadfoot, 1990.

Kinney, John Coddington. "Farragut at Mobile Bay." In *Battles and Leaders of the Civil War,* edited by Robert Underwood Johnson and Clarence Clough Buel. Vol. 4. 1887. Reprint, Secaucus, N.J.: Castle, n.d.

Liddell, St. John Richardson. *Liddell's Record.* Edited by Nathaniel C. Hughes. Dayton, Ohio: Morningside, 1985.

Macartney, Clarence Edward. *Mr. Lincoln's Admirals.* New York: Funk and Wagnalls, 1956.

Mahan, Alfred T. *Admiral Farragut.* New York; D. Appleton, 1892.

_____. *The Gulf and Inland Waters.* 1883. Reprint, Wilmington, N.C.: Broadfoot, 1989. These two works by the distinguished nineteenth-century naval historian are both worth reading.

Maury, Dabney Herndon. "The Defence of Mobile in 1865." *Southern Historical Society Papers* 3 (1877): 1–13. A brief account of the land battle by the commander of the Confederate forces.

Merriam, Henry C. "The Capture of Mobile." In *War Papers*, by the Maine Commandery of the Military Order of the Loyal Legion of the United States. Vol. 3. 1908. Reprint, Wilmington, N.C.: Broadfoot, 1992.

O'Connell, John C. "The Journal of Mr. John C. O'Connell, CSN, on the CSS *Tennessee.*" In *Two Naval Journals: 1864*, edited by C. Carter Smith Jr. Chicago: Wyvern Press of S. F. E., 1964. Another good first-hand account from inside the Confederate ram.

Page, Richard L. "The Defense of Fort Morgan." In *Battles and Leaders of the Civil War*, edited by Robert Underwood Johnson and Clarence Clough Buel. Vol. 4. 1887. Reprint, Secaucus, N.J.: Castle, n.d. An account by the commander of the fort.

Palfrey, John C. "The Capture of Mobile, 1865." In *Papers of the Military Historical Society of Massachusetts.* Vol. 8, *The Mississippi Valley, Tennessee, Georgia, Alabama, 1861–1864.* 1910. Reprint, Wilmington, N.C.: Broadfoot, 1989.

Parker, Foxhall A. *The Battle of Mobile Bay and the Capture of Forts Powell, Gaines, and Morgan.* Boston: A. Williams, 1878.

_____. "The Battle of Mobile Bay." In *Papers of the Military Historical Society of Massachusetts.* Vol. 12, *Naval Actions and History, 1799–1898.* 1902. Reprint, Wilmington, N.C.: Broadfoot, 1990.

Richmond Dispatch, January 12, 1900. This issue contains an appreciative obituary of Dabney Herndon Maury. It is reprinted in *Southern Historical Society Papers* 27 (1899): 335–49.

Ross, Fitzgerald. *Cities and Camps of the Confederate States.* Edited by Richard Barksdale Harwell. Urbana: University of Illinois Press, 1958.

Scharf, J. Thomas. *History of the Confederate States Navy from Its Organization to the Surrender of Its Last Vessel.* New York: Rogers and Sherwood, 1886.

Smith, Sidney Adair, and C. Carter Smith Jr., eds. *Mobile: 1861–1865.* Chicago: Wyvern Press of S.F.E., 1964.

Spears, John Randolph. *David G. Farragut.* Philadelphia: George W. Jacobs, 1905.

Stephenson, P.D. "Defence of Spanish Fort. On Mobile Bay—Last Great Battle of the War." *Southern Historical Society Papers* 39 (1914): 118–36. This is a very lively, readable, and useful account by a cannoneer in the besieged garrison.

Tarrant, Edward W. "After the Fall of Fort Blakely." *Confederate Veteran* 25 (April 1917): 152.

_____. "Siege and Capture of Fort Blakely." *Confederate Veteran* 23 (October 1915): 457–58.

Taylor, Richard. *Destruction and Reconstruction: Personal Experiences of the Late War.* 1879. Reprint, New York: Longmans, Green, 1955.

_____. "The Last Confederate Surrender." In *The Annals of the War Written by Leading Participants North and South.* 1878. Reprint, Dayton, Ohio: Morningside, 1988.

Thompson, Robert Means, and Richard Wainwright, eds. *Confidential Correspondence of Gustavus Vasa Fox, Assistant Secretary of the Navy, 1861–1865.* 2 vols. New York: Naval History Society, 1920.

U.S. Navy Department. *Official Records of the Union and Confederate Navies in the War of the Rebellion.* Ser. 1, vol. 21. 1906. Reprint, Harrisburg, Pa.: National Historical Society, 1987. This contains the official reports of the participants of the battle in the bay—an indispensable source.

U.S. War Department. *War of the Rebellion: Official Records of the Union and Confederate Armies.* 70 vols. in 128 parts. 1880–1901. Reprint, Harrisburg, Pa.: National Historical Society, 1971. The reports and correspondence of the land battle for Mobile are in ser. 1, vol. 49, pts. 1–2. Also an indispensable source.

Watson, J. Crittenden, and Joseph Marthon. "The Lashing of Admiral Farragut in the Rigging." In *Battles and Leaders of the Civil War,* edited by Robert Underwood Johnson and Clarence Clough Buel. Vol. 4. 1887. Reprint, Secaucus, N.J.: Castle, n.d.

Webster, Harrie. "An August Morning with Farragut at Mobile Bay." In *Civil War Naval Chronology, 1861–1865,* by the U.S. Navy Department. 6 parts. Washington, D.C.: Government Printing Office, 1961–66.

Wilson, John M. "The Campaign Ending with the Capture of Mobile." In *War Papers,* by the District of Columbia Commandery of the Military Order of the Loyal Legion of the United States. Vol. 1. 1894. Reprint, Wilmington, N.C.: Broadfoot, 1993.

Woodward, C. Vann, ed. *Mary Chesnut's Civil War.* New Haven: Yale University Press, 1981.

PHOTO CREDITS

We gratefully acknowledge the United States Military History Institute at Carlisle Barracks, Pennsylvania, for the photos of Franklin Buchanan, David G. Farragut, and Richard Taylor.

The images of Dabney Herndon Maury, James Alden, Edward R. S. Canby, Percival Drayton, Frederick Steele, Thornton A. Jenkins, James D. Johnston, Tunis A.M. Craven, James E. Jouett, Gordon Granger, Andrew Jackson Smith, Richard L. Page," "David Farragut and Percival Drayton," "Surrender of the *Tennessee*," "*Hartford* Engaging the *Tennessee*," "David Farragut and Gordon Granger," the USS *Hartford* and the CSS *Tennessee* are from Robert Underwood Johnson and Clarence Clough Buel, eds., *Battles and Leaders of the Civil War: Being For the Most Part Contributions by Union and Confederate Officers* (New York: Century Magazine, 1884-1887).

The picture "Union Troops Entering Mobile" is from Alfred H. Guernsey and Henry M. Alden, *Harper's Pictoral History of the Civil War* (Chicago: The Puritan Press Company, 1894).

PUBLISHER'S ACKNOWLEDGMENTS

The McWhiney Foundation Press would like to acknowledge the efforts of Daniel Price, a McWhiney Scholar, in the making of this book. He spent countless hours researching and writing many of the biographical sketches, collecting the photographs and illustrations, and compiling the appendices and index. We would also like to acknowledge Kevin Brock for his excellent copyediting work. Finally, we continue to be grateful to Henry Rosenbohm, of Rosenbohm Graphic Design, for his thoughtful and creative design of this and all of our Campaigns and Commanders Series books and covers.

INDEX

A

Adams, Myron, 56
Alabama River, *See* Rivers, major
Alabama, 72, 76, 80; *Pilot Town* 66
Alden, James, 32, 42, 43
Alden, John, 32
Anderson, Charles D., 63, 64, 65
Apalachee River, *See* Rivers, major
Arkansas Bluffs, 75
Arkansas, 26, 70, 72
Army of Northern Virginia, 16
Army of Tennessee, 71
Atlanta Campaign, *See* Civil War Campaigns
Atlantic fleet, 27, 29

B

Bay Shield Road, 87
Bayou Minette, 79
Brooke rifles, 21
Brother, Charles, 29, 31
Buchanan, Franklin (Buck), 21, 26, 29, 37, 40, 45, 48, 49, 50,
    51, 52, 53, 56, 57, 59

C

CSS *Gaines*, 21, 46
CSS *Morgan*, 21
CSS *Selma*, 21, 46
CSS *Tennessee*, 21, 22, 25, 26, 28, 29, 37, 38, 40, 42, 45, 46, 48,
    50, 52, 53, 55, 56, 57, 59, 60, 63
CSS *Virginia*, 50
Canby, Edward R. S., 67, 71, 72, 73, 74, 76, 77, 82, 84, 87, 88, 89
Chesnut, Mary, 67
Chickamauga, Battle of, 61
Civil War Campaigns, *Atlanta* 79; *Nashville* 79; *Red River* 26, 75
Civil War Forts, *Blakely* 18, 71, 73, 76, 77, 78, 79, 80, 84, 85;

Gaines 19, 20, 28, 63, 65, 67; *Leavenworth* 73; *Morgan*
19, 20, 22, 25, 26, 28, 31, 35, 37, 38, 44, 45, 48, 61, 63,
64, 65, 66, 67, 73; *Powell* 20, 66, 67; *Sumter* 73; *Spanish
Fort* 18, 71, 73, 76, 77, 78, 79, 81, 82, 83, 84, 85
Civil War Units, 13th Corps 73, 16th Corps 73, 76, 81,
Gibson's Louisiana brigade
Clark, Charles E., 57
Collins, Jean, 42
Conception Street, 87
Confederate States (Confederacy), 18, 19, 21, 22, 71, 77, 86, 89
Confederate Guns at Spanish Fort, *The Lady Gibson* 81, *The Lady
Slocum* 81, 82, *The Lady Maury* 81
Confederate States Navy, 21, 49, 65
Conrad, Daniel B., 29, 31, 42, 52, 57
Craven, T.A.M., 40, 41, 42

D
Dauphin Island, 19, 20, 28, 30, 60, 63
Davis, Jefferson, 88
Delaware, 76
Dixie, 89
Dog River, *See* Rivers, major
Dorn, Earl Van, 70
Drayton, Percival, 29, 30, 31, 36, 37, 40, 44, 48, 66

F
Farragut, David Glassgow, *prior to battle* 14, 15, 16, 20, 21, 22,
23, 25, 26, 27, 28, 29, 30, 31, 32, 34; *personal informa-
tion* 24; *preparation for battle* 35, 36, 37; *passing of the
forts* 38, 40, 42, 44, 45, 46, 48; *hunting the Tennessee*
49, 50, 53, 55, 56; *surrender of the ram* 60; *taking the
forts* 63, 65, 66, 67, 71
Florida Peninsula, 72
Florida, 72; *Pensacola* 29, 73, 76, 84, 87
Forrest, Nathan Bedford, 75
Fort Blakely, *See* Civil War Forts
Fort Gaines, *See* Civil War Forts

Fort Leavenworth, *See* Civil War Forts
Fort Morgan, *See* Civil War Forts
Fort Powell, *See* Civil War Forts
Fort Sumter, *See* Civil War Forts
Fox, Gustavus Vasa, 15
Freeman, Martin, 40, 44

G
Georgia, *Atlanta* 16
Gibson, Randall Lee, 79, 81, 82, 83, 84, 89
Grand Gulf battery, 29
Granger, Gordon, 28, 30, 31, 60, 61, 62, 63, 65, 66, 67, 73, 74, 87
Grant, Ulysses S., 71, 72, 85
Gray, John J., 85
Gulf District, 70
Gulf of Mexico, 15, 19, 29, 34, 35, 67, 75, 89
Guns, *See* Union Guns at Spanish Fort; Confederate Guns at
        Spanish Fort

H
Hail Columbia, 89
Hood, John B., 71
Hutchinson, William F., 38

J
Jenkins, Thornton Alexander, 28, 29, 30
Johnny Reb, 81
Johnston, James D., 37, 48, 52, 53, 56, 57, 59
Johnston, Joseph E., 87, 89
Jouett, James Edward, 42, 43, 44, 46

K
Kinney, John Coddington, 31, 55, 56

L
Le Roy, William E., 59, 60
Lee, Robert E., 16, 65, 77, 85, 87, 88

Liddell, St. John R., 77, 78, 79, 84, 85
Louisiana, 72, 79; *New Orleans* 14, 16, 24, 52, 65, 67

M
Magnolia Race Course, 87
Mahan, Dennis Hart, 70
Marchand, J.B., 54
Maury, Dabney Herndon, 67, 68, 69, 70, 71, 73, 76, 77, 78, 80,
    82, 83, 84, 86, 87, 88, 89
Maury, John Minor, 68
Maury, Matthew Fontaine, 69
Mayflower ship, 32
McAlester, M.D., 38
Mexican War, 29
Mississippi fleet, 27
Mississippi River, *See* Rivers, major
Mississippi Sound, 20
Mississippi, 72, 75; *Corinth* 75; *Cuba* 87; *Jackson* 75;
    Meridian 87, 89; *Vicksburg* 18, 75
Missouri, 72
Mobile Bay, 14, 16, 21, 24, 32, 34, 50, 65, 71, 80
Mobile Point, 19, 66
Mobile River, *See* Rivers, major
Mobile, Alabama, 15, 16, 18, 19, 22, 29, 49, 52, 66, 67, 70, 71,
    72, 73, 77, 78, 79, 82, 84, 85, 86, 87, 88
Murphey, Peter U., 46, 48

N
Nashville Campaign, *See* Civil War Campaigns
Navajos, 73
New Mexico Territory, 71, department of 73; *Santa Fe* 73
New York City, New York, 71
North Carolina, 89

P
Page, Richard Lucian, 38, 64, 65, 66
Pea Ridge, Battle of, 70

Pelican Island Spit, 63
Perry, Matthew C., 52
Port Hudson battery, 29

R
Red River Campaign, *See* Civil War Campaigns
Regiments, 21st Alabama 64
Rio Grande, *See* Rivers, major
Rivers, major, *Alabama River* 16, 22, 87; *Apalachee River* 18, 79;
    Dog River 26; *Mississippi River* 15; *Mobile River* 18; *Rio
    Grande* 15, 72; *Tombigbee River* 18, 87
Rosecrans, William, 61, 62

S
Sand Island, 31, 34
Seddon, John, 67
Selma, Alabama, 22
Sheridan, Philip H., 72
Sherman, William T., 72, 87, 89
Slough, R.H., 86
Smith, Andrew Jackson, 73, 74, 75, 84
Spanish Fort, *See* Civil War Forts
States, *See* individual state names
Steele, Frederick, 73, 74, 76, 84, 85

T
Taylor, Richard, 71, 77, 88, 89
Tennessee, 24; *Nashville* 75
Texas, 15, 26, 72
Thatcher, Henry K., 73
Thomas, George, 62
Thome, W.H., 81
Tombigbee River, *See* Rivers, major
Tower Island, 20
Trans-Mississippi West, 70

U

USS *Brooklyn*, 32, 35, 37, 38, 42, 44
USS *Chickasaw*, 27, 56, 57, 59
USS *Congress*, 50
USS *Cumberland*, 50
USS *Galena*, 36, 45
USS *Hartford*, 25, 29, 31, 32, 34, 35, 40, 42, 44, 45, 46, 48, 53, 54, 55, 56, 57, 59
USS *Itasca*, 36, 46
USS *Kennebec* , 35, 46
USS *Lackawanna*, 35, 38, 53, 55, 56, 57
USS *Merrimac*, 50
USS *Metacomet*, 35, 42, 45, 46
USS *Monitor*, 50
USS *Monongahela*, 35, 46, 53, 57
USS *Octorara*, 35
USS *Oneida*, 36, 45
USS *Ossipee*, 35, 57, 59
USS *Port Royal*, 35, 46
USS *Richmond* , 29, 31, 35
USS *Seminole*, 35
USS *Susquehanna*, 52
USS *Tecumseh* , 27, 29, 31, 37, 38, 40, 41, 42, 43
USS *Winnebago*, 27
USS *Manhattan*, 27, 41, 42
Union Guns at Spanish Fort, *Anna Maria* 81, *Sarah Jane* 81, *Elizabeth Ann* 81
United States Naval Academy, 52
United States Navy, 16, 25, 49, 52, 65, 68
United States of America (Union), 16, 62, 66, 67, 71, 75, 76, 86, 89
University of Louisiana, *Law Department* 79

V

Virginia, 68, 73; *Appomattox* 77, 85, 87; *Farragut* 34; *Hampton Roads* 50; *Petersburg* 77; *Richmond* 16, 67, 73

W
War Department, 15
War of 1812, 24
Waring, Mary, 86, 87
Washington, D.C., 15, 16
Watson, J. Crittenden, 44
Webster, Harrie, 41, 42
West Gulf Blockading Squadron, 16, 73
West Point, 70, 72
Wharton, A.D., 40
Whiting, J.W., 38

Y
Yale College, 79
Yankee Doodle, 87